Gold Diggers of the Klondike
Prostitution in Dawson City, Yukon, 1898–1908

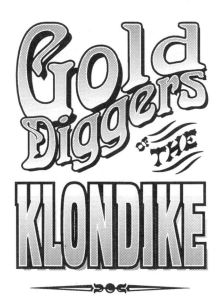

BAY RYLEY

Cover design by Terry Gallagher/Doowah Design
Author photo by Jenny Levitt

All photos and illustrations courtesy of the National Archives of Canada unless otherwise noted.

Published with the assistance of the Manitoba Arts Council and The Canada Council for the Arts

Printed and bound in Canada

Canadian Cataloguing in Publication Data

Ryley, Bay, 1970–
        Gold-diggers of the Klondike: prostitution in
Dawson City, Yukon, 1898–1908

Includes bibliographical references and index.
ISBN 1-896239-29-3

        1. Prostitution—Yukon Territory—Dawson—History.
2. Dawson (Yukon)—History. 3. Klondike River Valley
(Yukon)—Gold discoveries. 4. Yukon Territory—
History—1895–1918. I. Title.

HQ150.D38R95 1997   306.74'2'097191   C97-901236-8

Acknowledgments

I am indebted to many people in Whitehorse who offered accommodation, friendship, and advice during my time in the Yukon. Thanks especially to Lucy van Oldenbarneveld, Melissa Simpson, Yodit Johnson, Laura Cabott, Helen Voogd, Mike King, Mary-el Kerr and Doug Rody, Lois Moorcroft, Margaret McCullough, and José Janssen.

Several Yukon archivists and historians aided my research: those at the Yukon Archives, the Dawson City Museum and Historical Society, Canadian Parks Service (particularly David Neufeld), and the Northern Research Institute.

This book could not have been written without financial support. Thank you to the School of Graduate Studies and Research and the Department of History at Queen's University, the Department of Indian and Northern Affairs, and the Yukon Foundation.

I am grateful for the guidance I received from my professors at Queen's University. Nancy Forestell and Karen Dubinsky, my graduate supervisor, deserve the highest praise. Gordon Shillingford, the publisher and editor of this book, has been wonderfully kind and professional.

I also have many friends to thank for motivating me. Dave Seglins deserves special mention. Finally, my brothers, sisters, nieces, nephews and especially my parents, have all been incredibly supportive of me and my work, despite the shady subject matter.

Table of Contents

Introduction

> I have read something about this dance-hall in
> magazines.... There are accounts of painted dancers
> and other ladies who were present as an adjunct to
> such an establishment...and now this dance-hall,
> or theatre as the minister prefers to call it, has been
> declared an historical site, a shrine, or a monument
> and I want to know why.
> —House of Commons *Debates*, 22 March 1962
> (Opposition member's question regarding the
> proposed reconstruction of the Palace Grand
> Theatre to attract tourists to Dawson)

When the Diefenbaker government began prospecting for
tourists to renew a fading Dawson City, Yukon, they chose
to restore what must surely be the most lascivious of
Canadian national historic sites—a dance-hall from the
Klondike gold rush. For a brief but tantalizingly exciting
time, the Palace Grand echoed raucous laughter and the
clink of poker chips and champagne glasses, as miners in
from the creeks squandered their gold poke on gambling
and dance-hall girls.

The reconstruction of the Palace Grand Theatre in 1962
was the first of several elaborate federal government
initiatives to restore what was once the largest city west of
Winnipeg. Today, Dawson City is a full-scale tourist town
that invites tourists to "relive those brash exciting times"
of the gold rush. The Palace Grand offers a vaudeville-
style Gaslight Follies reminiscent of the turn-of-the-century

shows that early Dawsonites saw. Likewise, tourists can gamble and "enjoy the same kind of honky tonk entertainment with can-can girls and elaborately costumed chanteuses" at Diamond Tooth Gertie's Gambling Hall.[1] Visitors are welcome to peruse the cabins of authors Robert Service and Jack London. There, readings from "The Spell of the Yukon" and *Call of the Wild* offer a respite from the "racier" tourist attractions, and serve as a reminder that the gold rush was also about courageous men struggling against the elements of the far North.

What themes are projected from this interpretation of the Yukon's history? For one, the heavy emphasis on the gold rush has had the effect of leaving the histories of First Nations peoples on the periphery. It suggests (entirely inaccurately) that history began when non-Aboriginal people flocked to the Klondike in search of gold. Further, this story of brave men battling the Yukon wilderness, striking gold claims, drinking, gambling, and taming brazen dance-hall girls tells an explicitly sexual tale of the gold rush. As the official symbol of contemporary Dawson City, the can-can girl, of course, is the representative of this wantonness.

Today can-can dancers grace local and "outside" events alike. Tourism-induced or not, there is a strong allegiance to the glory days of the gold rush in the Yukon. The editor of the *Yukon News* learned this the hard way when he printed an editorial entitled "It's Time to Can the Can-Can Dancers" in March 1992. Acknowledging that he was disparaging a Yukon institution, Peter Lesniak suggested that the Yukon "disband this talentless group of thick-thighed hoofers (heifers) now" since "as we all know, can-can dancers doubled as whores during the Klondike Gold Rush. Their little (in the artistic sense) musical numbers were used to disguise how they really earned their earnings."[2]

"Protesters Demand Editor's Resignation," read the front page of the *Yukon News* the next day. Carrying signs and forming a can-can line outside the building, 150 demonstrators protested Lesniak's remarks. A barrage of letters to the editor ensued, some entitled "Don't Shoot Down Our Ambassadors," "Don't Slam Yukon Traditions," and "Article Undermines the Yukon's Heritage." Remarks about "thick thighs" irked many, but it was the fact that the can-can is regarded as an important part of Yukon history that was the focus of the complaints.

One doesn't wish to sabotage local lore, but the fact is that myth rarely reproduces authenticity. Some confusion exists about the sordid aspects of the gold rush. Can-can girls, it seems, have been mistaken for the dance-hall girls, who danced with men and were paid commission on the drinks sold in the dance-halls. It is possible that the can-can was performed in theatres such as the Opera House, the Monte Carlo, and the Palace Grand, in which there were vaudeville and other shows, but evidence of this is scant. More likely, the can-can girls did not take to the stage until at least the late1960s, when Dawson began prospecting for summer tourists by highlighting its exciting gold rush past.

Dawson City is hardly the only place in Canada to shape history into a tourist attraction. Across the country there is a plethora of military forts, pioneer villages, and other vestiges of a recreated past that offer a history lesson in exchange for tourist dollars. It should be no surprise that occasional liberties are taken with the facts in order to increase entertainment value. The June 1997 celebration of the 500th anniversary of John Cabot's ship landing in Newfoundland is but one example. The event brought many visitors to Newfoundland, but the question of whether the *Matthew* ever actually graced the shores of Bonavista is a subject of some debate.

By placing selective persons and events in the spotlight, places earn reputations that they become readily associated with. Calgary has its stampede, Prince Edward Island has its famous but fictitious Anne of Green Gables, and the Yukon has its Klondike gold rush. The fascinating issue is not so much the accuracy of every detail, but the way the story is told.

Not everyone agrees on the rightful place of the can-can girl in Yukon history. In some circles there is a distinct uneasiness about the fact that she has taken centre stage. Some argue that the "whoop it up school of history"—the romance and legend of the gold rush—should be taken with a grain of salt.[3] Too much attention has been paid to the prostitutes and dance-hall girls at the expense of Klondike women whose experience was "banal rather than scandalous," others assert.[4] Certainly there is a need to recognize that most women who travelled to the Klondike were not members of "the oldest profession." However, before we strike all women of ill repute from the historical record, or boo the can-can girls off the stage, it is worth investigating their eminence further. That is one of the purposes of the book: to shed some light on the women of the Klondike gold rush who—until now—have not been given serious consideration.

The prostitutes are not the sole actors in this story of vice in the Klondike. It takes two to tango, of course, and the men who visited the prostitutes also require some attention. According to Robert Service, it seemed that "the spirit of degeneracy" during the gold rush afflicted all:

> Cases in Court had to be adjourned because of the debauches of lawyers. Bank tellers stepped into their cages sleepless from all night orgies. Government officials lived openly with wanton women.... Fathers of families paraded the streets arm in arm with demi-mondaines.[5]

It is safe to assume that this is an embellishment. In fact, the men who frequented the demimonde were protected by a cloak of privacy and discretion in a way that the demi-mondaines were not. Nevertheless, it is still possible to eke out some information about these men, as Chapter 3 does.

Other men profited from, rather than paid for, their association with the "scarlet women." The pimps—known as "macques" in Dawson—are the focus of Chapter 4. However, living off the avails of prostitution was not confined to the macques—the men who bore the brunt of social stigma. Many prominent men—including land owners, real estate agents, and even politicians—profited from vice during the gold rush.

Of course then, as now, prostitution was illegal, though the authorities took a flexible approach to the crime. The regulation of prostitution changed significantly over time. Prostitution was considered a necessary aspect of a mining town where single men were in the vast majority. Medical inspection of prostitutes for venereal disease, as well as the establishment of a "red light" district, demonstrated that the official policy toward prostitution was one of tolerance at the height of the rush.

This "wide open" policy would only last so long. By 1899 southern moral reformers and, subsequently, the federal government, condemned Dawson's official tolerance of prostitution. Chapter 5 demonstrates that Ottawa's complaints were about much more than prostitution. Vice provided the ammunition in several underlying battles between the Laurier government and the administrators of the Yukon.

By 1902, Dawson's "respectable" citizens were prepared to take moral matters into their own hands. Chapter 6 chronicles the crackdown on prostitution. In post-rush Dawson, flagrant prostitution was incompatible with what was becoming a more settled and "civilized" (though economically shrinking) community. It is suggested here that this campaign against "immorality" was also a symptom of, and a reaction to, the economic woes plaguing Dawson as the boom times waned.

The final chapter exposes a 1908 anti-vice campaign by a Presbyterian minister from the Klondike. In doing so, it reiterates a larger theme of this book: that moral concerns are malleable and have no real "expiry date." Ten years after the gold rush, Dawson was hardly deserving of Reverend John Pringle's desclaration that the town was an "open and offensive moral sewer." However, such accusations still had the power to stir emotions and ignite political debate. Ironically, the gambling and dance-halls that were once the bane of respectable Dawson are today the celebrated features of the Yukon tourism industry.

CHAPTER 1

A Brief History
of the Klondike Gold Rush

The Klondike gold rush was the peak of a series of gold discoveries in western North America that began in California in 1849. The first gold discovered in Canada's Pacific region was in the Queen Charlotte Islands in 1842, and in 1858 a more significant find occurred on the Fraser River. After the 1858 discovery, about 25,000 people came to British Columbia, many of whom were Americans who had been in California during its gold rush. Two years later gold was discovered near Cariboo Lake, then in 1861 on the Stikine River, and, continuing north, in 1871 in the Cassiar district of northern B.C.

Since the 1880s people had been prospecting for gold in the Klondike River and its tributaries. They were in search of alluvial gold that could be panned for in the creeks. It was an enormous strike in August of 1896 by George Carmacks, a Californian, and two Tagish Indian brothers, Dawson Charlie and Skookum Jim, that prompted the famous Klondike gold rush. There was quite a gap in time, however, between the strike at Bonanza Creek and the moment when the rest of the world was made aware of it.

It was not until July of 1897—nearly a year after the discovery—that the tremendous strike in the Yukon became international news. On July 14, 1897, the *Excelsior* landed in San Francisco carrying over $500,000 worth of gold

(1897 standard). Two days later, the *Portland* docked in Seattle with sixty-eight miners carrying over $1 million worth of gold.[1] It was really these events that prompted the Klondike gold rush of 1898. The news of the gold-filled ships captured worldwide media attention. Thousands of people from all over North America, Europe, and beyond began packing their bags and heading for the Yukon. The gold rush was a welcome relief during a great depression. As one historian has remarked, "the discovery of seemingly unlimited quantities [of gold], waiting in the frozen streams to be picked up by anyone who could be bothered bending over, seemed to conform to men's hopes of a new period of prosperity."[2]

There were a few routes to the Klondike, but the shortest, least expensive, and most popular one was to take a steamer up the Pacific coast to Skagway or Dyea, Alaska. This was followed by an arduous hike over the Chilkoot Pass to the headwaters of the Yukon River. The stampeders who came in search of gold were hardly the first to set foot on this land, however. Rarely is there recognition that as treacherous as the Chilkoot trek was, the trail was not blazed by gold-seekers, but had been an inland trade route for the coastal Tlingit for thousands of years prior to the flood of non-aboriginal people to the Yukon. As the stampeders set out on the trail with their minimum one ton of goods, the Tagish and Tlingit peoples eased the heavy load for those headed for the Klondike gold fields. First Nations men, women, and children were employed as packers over the trail before the completion of the White Pass railway in 1899.[3]

Overall, the gold rush was devestating for the aboriginal population. When the gold-seekers made it to Dawson, they displaced the Hän from their traditional fishing grounds at the convergence of the Yukon and Klondike Rivers. The stampeders evicted some of the Hän from their cabins in what later became known as Klondike City—a "suburb" of Dawson. Along with their zest for gold, the newcomers brought diseases that claimed the lives of many

Yukon First Nations peoples. The huge influx of people also depleted game and timber in the areas around Dawson.

Few of the Hän received any economic benefit from the gold rush. Some Hän men worked as woodcutters or deck hands on steamers. Others sold meat and fish.[4] Women could sew, cook, or provide laundry services for the mining community, but most remained outside of the wage-labour economy altogether. The Hän were aware of the presence of gold for jundreds of years, yet as soon as it "claimed" and given market value, gold was kept out of reach of Yukon First Nations. First Nations peoples were not persuaded by officials to sign treaties or to live on reserves as they were in other parts of Canada in case gold should be discovered on this land.[5] Further, labour policies excluded the Hän from employment in placer mining.

Though the disastrous effect of the gold rush on First Nations peoples was long-lasting, the rush itself was short-lived. By the time that most people arrived in the Yukon in late spring of 1898, the actual gold strike was two years past. There was still gold to be prospected, but the best claims had already been staked. Disillusioned, many stampeders left the Yukon. Some found opportunities in providing a range of services necessary to sustain the mining community, and others took on labouring jobs. As early as January 1898, Clifford Sifton (federal Minister of the Interior) enacted new regulations that approved twenty-year dredging leases to be authorized to large corporations, most of whom bought out the original claim owners. At this point, consolidated mining companies such as the Treadgold and the Guggenheim came to dictate the economy of the Yukon, and day labour began to replace grubstaking on the creeks.

An official census for the Yukon was not taken until 1901, but most estimates agree on a maximum population of 40,000 for 1898. In 1901, the population of the Yukon was about 27,000. About one-third of the people were in Dawson itself and most of the rest of the non-aboriginal population were on the Klondike creeks. Dawson experienced a steady population decline after the rush. Many gold-seekers left in 1899 when gold was discovered in Nome, Alaska. A large strike in 1903 in the Tanana River drew even more to Fairbanks, where the belief was that individual prospectors still had a chance to strike it rich.[6]

Over the ten-year period covered by this book, the Klondike region underwent a major transformation. The indigenous population was disrupted by the flood of stampeders. For a time, Dawson was a subarctic city filled with people from around the world seeking their fortune. It is to the people and politics of the Klondike gold rush that we will now turn our attention.

CHAPTER 2

A View of the Demi-Monde: Profile of Klondike Prostitutes

> At the back doors of the tiny frame houses, the whores, laughing and singing, calling out to each other and chattering like bright birds, were making their toilets for the evening. Some were washing their long hair—invariably bright gold or jet black—drying it in the sun and leisurely brushing it out. Others were just reclining languorously and gossiping with their friends.[1]

This was how well-known middle-class Dawsonite Laura Berton described the scene of "unparalleled gaiety" from a plateau directly above Lousetown, while on a risky venture to examine the goings-on in ignoble Klondike City. Presumably a romanticized version, Berton's account exemplifies the distant views from "above"—newspaper accounts, court reports and records, and the North-West Mounted Police (NWMP) convict register—that comprise the sources upon which this book must rely.

Although the presence of prostitutes in the Klondike is exhaustively chronicled in popular histories and memoirs, there are few references to any individual women, aside from dance-hall celebrities like Klondike Kate and Diamond Tooth Gertie. They are immortalized as the names of present-day establishments in Dawson—a restaurant and a casino, respectively. Trite anecdotes and superficial commemoration have had to stand in for more accurate information about Klondike prostitutes and dance-hall girls—a symptom of the fact that this highly transient group rarely left written records of their daily life. Acknowledging this as a limitation, it is still possible to reconstruct a profile of the women engaged in prostitution in what was once the most notorious region of Canada.

Reports from the Klondike gold fields circulated worldwide. Revelry and its associated "sins" were frequently mentioned in newspaper articles, magazine stories, and travel guides. Even before Dawson's own expressed concern about the flagrant women of Dawson, southern moral reformers declared their disapproval of what was initially a more relaxed attitude toward regulating prostitution in the Yukon. The Women's Christian Temperance Union (WCTU), as we shall see, wrote to two members of Parliament when they caught wind that "profligate women" had free rein in Dawson.

What was unusual about these letters was that they focussed on the depravity of the women. Normally the WCTU emphasized *male* vice when campaigning against immorality.[2] At their Sixth World Convention in 1898, the WCTU pledged themselves to "tenderest sympathy with and active work for those of our sisterhood who have lost the priceless jewel of virtue, knowing them to be more sinned against than sinning."[3] Why was it that the "sinned against" part of the equation—so prevalent in urban North America[4]—was absent in the Yukon during this period?

At least part of the reason was the extent of the journey the women travelled in order to ply their trade. This suggests a degree of intent that was less apparent in urban prostitution. Big cities, it was believed at the time, lured innocent women from rural towns into urban debauchery.[5] Rather than having been unsuspectingly *lured* to the subarctic, however, Dawson prostitutes appeared to have made a concerted and calculated effort to get there, knowing full well of the employment opportunities available to them in the Yukon. As one commentator posed it: "I never heard of a girl 'going to the bad' in Dawson. Any woman who went to the bad in Dawson had, from all appearances, been there before and was quite familiar with the primrose way."[6]

Just as many of the men who came to the Klondike had been following other gold and mineral rushes in the western United States and Canada, so too had many women. The occupation of Kitty Henry (who was arrested on March 29, 1902) was listed in the police gaol record as "following mining camps," in Colorado, Cripple Creek, "etc." Similarly, Louise Coragaud left Paris in 1901 and, after a one-month sojourn in the hard-rock mining town of Butte, Montana, arrived in Dawson in 1902.[7]

Numerous women were prostitutes by occupation who, as transients, had plied their trade in many urban centres. Maggie Johnson, for instance, maintained herself by prostitution over the time she lived in Minnesota, Vancouver, Seattle, and—for the four or five years prior to her arrest in 1903—Dawson City. Others came and went from the Klondike, as the seasons or other factors prescribed. Elizabeth Brooks (alias Slavis) immigrated to New York from Germany as a girl. Since then, she had resided in Minnesota and Colorado (where she met her husband Frank) before arriving in Dawson in 1898. She left the Yukon in 1899, returned in June 1901, and was arrested as an inmate of a house of ill fame a year later at the age of thirty-seven.

"Those Females With Black Bart Proclivities"

The depiction of prostitutes and dance-hall girls as being cunning and aggressive also had origins in their connection to the world of crime and petty thievery. One of the more extreme members of the demimonde was Lulu Watts, a one-time Dawson dance-hall girl. In July of 1900, Watts was charged with assault. She was not satisfied with the service that she and her two male friends had received in a restaurant, so Watts hit the proprietor over the head with a bottle.[8] Less than two years later Lulu Watts was living in Nome, Alaska. It was there that she killed Jack Kirk with a hatchet as he slept in a room above the Gold Belt dance-hall. Immediately following the murder, the dance-hall girl attempted suicide by jumping into the Bering Sea from the beachside Gold Belt.[9]

Committing murder was rare, but prostitutes and dance-hall girls were frequently accused of theft. Eva Edmilson (alias Terry) and Della Hunter were considered "very naughty young females." The two prostitutes were sentenced to two and a half years and eighteen months in jail, respectively, for robbing Isaac Ogren of $280 at the Seattle Hotel. After drinking with him in the bar, Edmilson and Hunter accompanied Ogren to an upstairs room where, at some point that night, his pockets were emptied. Twenty-nine-year-old Edmilson was known to have "habitually consorted with thieves and pickpockets"; this was why she was given a longer jail sentence than her accomplice. Over the two years prior to her conviction, Minnesota-born Eva Edmilson had circulated between Dawson, Nome, Alaska, and Seattle, Washington three times. She was described in the gaol record as being tall and "strong looking," with a "long face, aquiline nose and wide hips." Della Hunter—her less-seasoned, twenty-seven-year old accomplice—was born in New York state. She had worked in Minneapolis, Minnesota and Portland, Oregon before making the trek to Dawson in March 1902. She was "stout" and "determined looking," according to the NWMP. The two had been planning a getaway. Two tickets for Whitehorse, a cheque for $250, and $62 cash were found in Hunter's pocket at the time of her arrest.[10]

Another duo of thieving prostitutes, Maggie Johnson (alias Richardson) and Maud Westwood (alias "Australian Maud") , were sentenced to six months in jail for stealing $110 in gold dust from Edward Cairns. On a winter's night in 1903, Cairns met Maggie Johnson on the road to Grand Forks, and, as he testified, "recognized her as a kind of a sporting woman." Cairns then checked into the Gold Hill Hotel with Johnson, introducing her as his wife. The couple—along with Johnson's friend Maud Westwood—proceeded to get drunk in the hotel room. Later that night, the threesome visited "Australian Maud's" place—a notorious house of ill repute. At some point during the night's carousing, the two women had collaborated on the robbery, Cairns insisted. The NWMP felt the need to record that Johnson, who was born in Redwing, Minnesota, had a "foreign appearance," a "sallow" complexion, and "irregular, rough, and badly kept fingernails."[11]

Jennie Mack (who had three aliases) was handed a two-year prison sentence for stealing $600 cash from George Blondo at the Gold Bottom Hotel in October 1902. Apparently, this dance-hall girl, prostitute, and keeper of the Pioneer Lodging House was a "dangerous and unscrupulous woman." Jennie Mack was born in New York and had lived in Ohio, Michigan, and Seattle before settling in Dawson. In court, Mack maintained that the real thief was a Mounted Police officer named Woods who had been previously discharged from the force for "drinking on duty and consorting with lewd women."[12]

These incidents of prostitutes supplementing their income by stealing from clients came to the attention of the NWMP. The police were "determined to put a stop now and for all time to the practice these harlots have of getting men drunk and then deliberately robbing them of everything they possess." The rationale for this was "not so much of a desire to make a Sunday town of the city" as it was a plan to "compel those females with Black Bart proclivities to seek pastures new."[13] But intentions of a "Sunday town" or not, by 1902 there was a determined effort to keep prostitutes beyond the limits of Dawson City. If a woman of ill repute was not arrested for her "Black Bart" proclivities, she would likely be fined or sentenced for prostitution-related offences.

When prostitution was tolerated (up until 1902), the *Klondike Nugget* regretted that "the social evil cannot be discussed in newspapers."[14] It usually refrained from naming individual women. Instead, the papers printed euphemisms for prostitutes and prostitution: "the scarlet letter," "the demi-monde," "the soiled doves," or "the tenderloin." It was not *until* 1902 that there were large-scale arrests and, concurrently, that prostitutes' names were a regular sight in the police-court column. Many women faced the law repeatedly. Alice Miller, Jeanette Benneau, Elizabeth Davis, Margaret Benoit, Margaret Mercier, Louise Coragaud, Lucille Martin and Marcelle Martin, Mignon Miller, and Virginia Olbrea, to name but a few, were all arrested at least twice in the crackdown of 1902. Some prostitutes' careers are traceable by records of their arrests, as are general trends in the regulation of prostitution.

One of the most resilient women may have been Margaret Mercier. Mercier was one of at least twenty-five women who were brought before the police court over a three-day period in April 1902 for operating cigar stores as subterfuges for houses of ill fame. As the "crusade against the women of the town"[15] continued, Margaret Mercier was among "a great show of furs and the rustle of silks" in police court a few months later. The women were said to have offered the judge "the coyest and sweetest of smiles" when Magistrate Macaulay suspended his sentence— provided that the women absolutely obey the law. Mercier, for one, did not take the judge's threat very seriously. With the assistance of "a man said to be her husband," Mercier ran the Fourth Avenue Hotel for several years. In February 1908 she was convicted twice for selling liquor in the house without a license.[16] Later the same month she was prosecuted for keeping a house—the Fourth Avenue Hotel—for the purposes of prostitution. Judge Craig held that Mercier's establishment was "offensive to the public and dangerous to the morals of the community."[17]

During the crackdown on prostitution, it was often varying combinations of the same women who were arrested. Being hauled into court together probably helped to maintain or create professional, if not personal, relationships. Lucille Martin, Marcelle Martin, and Louise Coragaud were French women who travelled to Dawson in 1902 as a group, along with John Robert and Felix Duplau—two macques. A year later, the three women plus Robert were arrested for "participating in exhibitions of a grossly indecent nature"[18] as the inmates of a notorious house of ill fame known as the Bartlett House.

Each of these Bartlett House inmates had previous confrontations with the law. The three women were arrested together on an earlier occasion in September 1902, when they were among twelve female keepers of disorderly houses in South Dawson who were brought to trial.[19] Lucille Martin and her sister Marcelle were two of twenty-five cigar store "merchants" arrested in April 1902.[20] The fact that Marcelle was "good looking" with a "well developed bust" did not escape the notice of the NWMP. Louise Coragaud (who spoke no English) was sentenced to a jail term for contempt of court in March 1902. She had refused to answer questions regarding Felix Duplau, who was charged with living off the avails of prostitution. A recent arrival from "gay Paris," Coragaud had a "strong will" and "no amount of questioning could induce her to give a direct answer."[21]

Once a woman was arrested on charges of prostitution, she was more easily identifiable to the NWMP officers who pursued prostitutes in the course of duty. Constable Mallett witnessed Margaret Benoit standing in the alleyway leading to her home and talking with different men late at night, and claimed to have seen "men go into her cabin and stay for a short time and come out again" in April 1903. This was not the constable's first exposure to this "woman of shady reputation,"[22] however. Eight months earlier Mallett was chastised at Benoit and Pauline Berge's successful appeal to the territorial court for arresting them without sufficient evidence. Mallett had failed to apprehend the women while they were in the midst of soliciting clients. "I tried to, but [they] evaded me by dodging around from one street to the other," he told the court.[23]

Sexual Commerce

For Klondike prostitutes, contending with NWMP officers and lawmakers was a trick of the trade. According to some, however, this was small penance to pay for what was regarded as a very lucrative line of work. In one NWMP Inspector's estimation, women were attracted by the "glare and glitter and a life of...luxury as compared with the lives of their hard working and honest sisters."[24] By 1899, greed had already caught up with dance-hall women, opined the *Dawson Daily News*: "In the good old days of '96, '97, and '98, the dance-hall queen cared not so much for personal adornment, but rather prided herself on her staying powers for drink and revelry."

The notion that gold-mining community prostitutes were capitalizing women was echoed in many books and memoirs published after the gold rush:

A thousand ounces of rich virgin gold, fresh-won from the Klondike creek beds, could nightly flow into 'the girls' capacious pockets, and still they could find ways of spending more in a meretricious grandeur. No wonder that purveyors of fine Paris frocks flourished in Dawson, and jewellers sent Outside for shipments of the largest diamonds available.[25]

For Marcelle Martin, Lucille Martin, and Louise Coragaud—the denizens of the infamous Bartlett House—their wealth was no mere invention. Following their sentence to two months of hard labour, the contents of the Bartlett House were auctioned off. Included in the list of items were "parlour sets of the latest style from Paris," decorated chamber sets, an assortment of gold jewellery and diamond rings, and "numerous other fancy articles."[26] The women raised enough money to pay the $3,000 bail for John Robert—the "macque" of the Bartlett House—who was charged with living off the avails of their toil.

Working out of a house of ill repute may have been more profitable than streetwalking, but that too could reap an income. A judge asked Constable Wright whether Margaret Benoit and Pauline Berge gave him any explanation of what they were doing on the streets of Dawson. "Yes, they said they were screwing for $3," he replied.[27] In "one of the raciest cases probably ever tried in the Yukon," Lucy Miller testified that from July to December, 1898 she earned between $10 and $20 a night. The average wage for a male miner on the creeks, it should be noted, was $10 a day in 1898.[28]

The lengthy career of May Fields—"a well known notorious character around town"—provided a significant income as well as the ownership of some property. At her July 1908 trial for being the keeper of a bawdy-house on Fourth Avenue and a "loose, idle, and disorderly person," she testified that she had been in Dawson for ten years.[29] Fields arrived a newlywed, but after her husband left her in 1900, she had worked in the dance-halls. Denying the charge against her she said: "I am making my own living. I have two cabins that I rent for $60 a month and I work in the [Orpheum] dance-hall." When asked about her income from the dance-hall, Fields stated that she earned between $8 and $20 per night. This was progress—four years earlier she had been a tenant occupying "a fine suite" of Rooms 1 and 2 at the Royal Hotel.[30]

Grace Rogers, Flo Harper, and Louise Sullivan (dance-hall women from the M&N) were earning enough to plan for their retirement on the shores of Lake Laberge. In 1903, the three "spinsters" (according to the 1901 census) applied to the Crown Timber and Land agent for three adjacent 160-acre lots. This land was miles from the din of the Klondike dance-halls where they worked. Unfortunately, a 1905 letter from the agent cancelled their application because they had not complied with its terms; either they had failed to make payments or they had left the territory altogether.[31]

Many dance-hall women never made the move from

the dance floor to the bedroom, but the association of prostitution with the dancehalls was a touchy subject even years after the rush. The famous Klondike Kate made efforts to set her (clean) record straight nearly four decades after her debut at the Palace Grand Theatre. In a 1937 interview with the *Seattle Post-Intelligencer*, Mrs. Kate Rockwell Matson of Bend, Oregon chided the "present-day fictioneers and motion picture producers" who "grossly libelled them." Rockwell maintained: "We weren't fallen women. Sure we worked for percentages on the liquor checks, but it stopped there. People nowadays have got the old-time dance-hall girls mixed up with the girls who lived across the river." Described by the reporter as "an eminently respectable and charming person herself," Mrs. Kate Rockwell Matson "spends her winters in the beautiful town of Bend, where she is extremely active in civic, social and Catholic circles."[32]

Without casting aspersions on Klondike Kate, there exists considerable evidence that the two occupations were indeed conflated for many women. Working out of a dance-hall could even provide a refuge from being convicted of prostitution. Sergeant McMillan found it difficult to prosecute women from the Flora Dora in 1907. "They all have the reputation of being Prostitutes," he explained, "but while they are allowed to be employed in the Dance hall they do not come under the Vagrancy Act, and it is very hard to get the necessary evidence to convict them of prostitution."[33] And regardless of whether these dance-hall girls were prostitutes on the side, the act of receiving a percentage of drinks sales in payment for dancing with men must be considered a form of sexual commerce.

On July 18, 1900, Z.T. Wood, commander of the NWMP, was asked to furnish Commissioner Ogilvie with the numbers of prostitutes, dance-hall girls, and gamblers residing in Dawson. Wood counted forty-nine prostitutes, and he also reported, "There are forty-two dance-hall girls; 28 of these girls live over saloons, particularly the 'Criterion,' 'Green Tree,' and 'Pavilion' dance-hall. The remainder occupy cabins in different parts of the town."[34] For dance-hall girls who lived above their place of work, the proximity made moonlighting more convenient. Indeed, the 1902 amendment to the Liquor License Ordinance of 1899 suggests that efforts were being made to discourage such activity. Section 61 ordered that "No hotel or saloon licensee shall permit any person to occupy any room or other part of his licensed premises if he suspects or has reason to believe that such person intends to use the same for any improper or immoral purpose, nor allow any female suspected of being a prostitute to occupy any room therein."[35]

John McCrimmon, the manager of the Orpheum dance-hall, had his employees sign a contract to prevent them from moonlighting:

> Each girl and woman is to appear on the Dance Hall floor at the hour of 9 o'clock every evening and to remain there continuously with the exception of such hours for meals as the manager may decide until the hour of 5 o'clock on the following morning and while inside the Dance Hall such woman and girl is to conduct herself in an orderly and respectable manner.... No girl shall absent herself from the Dance Hall between 9 o'clock and 5 o'clock without the consent from the manager.[36]

It is significant that this contract was used as evidence against May Fields when she was convicted of keeping a bawdy-house in 1908. In his direct examination of McCrimmon, Crown Prosecutor Pattullo sought to establish that dance-hall girls like Fields commonly doubled as prostitutes. He questioned why Lee Wilson, Mable White, Della Bean and Irene Brown's names were crossed off the contract. McCrimmon answered that either they had left Dawson to set up business in Klondike City (in Lee Wilson's case) or he had discovered they were prostitutes and fired them.

Regarding Fields in particular, Pattullo asked, "Take May Fields—did you ever hear whether her general reputation was that of a prostitute?" "No sir, not any more than any of the rest of the women," he replied. McCrimmon was fairly evasive in his testimony. When asked whether he had told Constable McCarvell that May Fields was using the dance-hall as "a stall; as a place to make appointments to take men home to her house," he conceded: "that is the way it looked to me or I would not have scratched her name off.... Lots of girls make appointments to go to cat with different gentlemen."[37]

The link between being a dance-hall girl and a prostitute was fairly obvious, but there may have been other occupations where women supplemented their earnings with prostitution. In the census from Klondike City—the suburb where many prostitutes moved after 1901—several women who had appeared in court for prostitution offences were enumerated as having "legitimate" occupations. These included dressmaker, tailor, laundress, and florist. It is possible that these women were concealing their life of prostitution from government officials. On the other hand, they may have had two part-time jobs. No one was ever sure about a woman named Ninon who had a shack with a dressmaker's sign within a few yards of the A.B. Hall. "As far as the Police are aware she is what she calls herself—a dressmaker," Inspector Wroughton noted, "though rumour has it, she is a prostitute." Many of these women did genuinely offer the services advertised. Sergeant McMillan visited a dressmakers shop and witnessed women waiting on customers with sewing needs. He knew them to be prostitutes, but was not concerned because "from their behaviour there is nothing to indicate to a stranger that they are women of that Class as they do not solicit in their store."[38]

Obviously for some women, prostitution afforded a means of accruing substantial amounts of capital. For others, it was only a slightly more lucrative occupation than being a laundress or dressmaker, or it provided temporary relief from poverty. Descriptions of extravagant lifestyles of these women detract from the reality that prostitutes and dance-hall girls were in a precarious occupation.

"Her bicycle pathway through life was strewn with carpet tacks"

Marie Chiviex and Dora Wells appeared in court "each looking as though her bicycle pathway through life was strewn with carpet tacks."[39] Subjective as this observation was, it may well have been warranted in this and other instances. The prostitutes of the Klondike faced unwanted pregnancy,[40] physical abuse, alcohol and drug dependency, and other such occupational hazards.

The ordeal of trekking to the gold fields of the Klondike and the rigorous life in the Yukon were thought to be fertile ground for insanity and suicide—although there is no indication that suicide was more common in the Yukon than in any other place. Early twentieth-century newspapers reported graphically detailed accounts of suicides, and the death of a dance-hall girl or prostitute provoked particular interest.

Stella Hill (born Kitty Straub) of Boon's Ferry, Oregon chose "death by the strychnine route" at the estimated age of nineteen or twenty years in December 1898. "The pressure of life within the Arctic region proved too much" for this dance-hall girl from the Monte Carlo. When Stella Hill went to the Pioneer Saloon to pick up Charley Hill (the bartender with whom she was living) after work, she was met with the news that led to her self-demise—he had left with another girl.[41] The motive for nineteen-year-old Myrtle Brocce's suicide in December of 1898 was even more simplified in the reportage. The dance-hall girl from the Tivoli had shot herself after reading a novel where the heroine had done the same.[42]

The tragic deaths of these young women provided the

rest of the community with an opportunity to speculate about the private lives of public women. Motives were created that were thought to suit their lifestyles. The financial problems, police harassment, illness, and social stigmatization that may have contributed to suicide attempts by prostitutes were never mentioned.[43]

Race, Ethnicity and Nationality

The majority of the scarlet women were from the United States (reflecting the fact that Americans were the largest group in the general population), but there was racial and ethnic diversity within the group. Occasionally prostitutes were singled out because of their colour:

> In Willie Wallis and Josephine Arnold, negro blood predominates, they being of a complexion which, away down south in the land of Dixie, would cause them to be referred to as 'smoked Yankees.'[44]

Referring to a May 1, 1901 NWMP order for all prostitutes to leave the city limits, the *Nugget* warned, "No dilly-dallying will be tolerated by the police as all must get out—whites, niggers and Japs, the colour line not being recognized in the order."[45]

Absent, though, from newspaper reports or any other form of documentation are references to First Nations women being prostitutes. It has been suggested that some Hän women engaged in prostitution before the rush, but that they were displaced by the numerous non-Aboriginal women who came north during the rush.[46] An historian of the pre-rush period documents that at the very least, Hän women made leisure in mixed company possible for non-Aboriginal men. The memoirs of a newcomer to Fortymile, for instance, described "squaw dances," where a small group of Hän women arrived at a local saloon, each with a baby on her back. As the fiddle started, "some of the most reckless miners grabbed an Indian woman and began furiously swinging her around in a sort of waltz, while the others crowded around and looked on."[47] This scene gives an indication of the extent to which the quest for gold disrupted the lives of First Nations people in the Klondike region.

Evidently, there is no universal depiction of the Dawson prostitute or dance-hall girl. What all had in common, however, was that their activities were heavily scrutinized by the police and by "respectable" citizens of Dawson. This, as we shall see, was not the case for the male callers who knocked on the doors and rapped on the windows of the demi-monde.

CHAPTER 3

Consorting with Prostitutes: Men and the Necessary Evil

> It is a remarkable fact and a tribute to the refining influence of the members of the gentler sex that since their arrival in Dawson the tone of the camp has undergone a decided change.... When men are isolated entirely from the society of women they become careless as to their appearance and neglectful of themselves. It is the potent spell of the name "woman" that restores them to a proper appreciation of the proprieties of life.[1]
> —1898 *Klondike Nugget* editorial celebrating the arrival of greater numbers of "respectable women."

Just as the presence of women was presumed to be a "refining influence," an unusually high surplus of men was regarded as a potential source of social disorder. Much of the history written about the northern and western frontiers of North America reflects this notion. Instant railway towns on the Canadian Prairies that attracted large groups of single men, for example, were apparently a prescription for prostitution. In *Red Lights on the Prairies*, James H. Gray describes Regina (c. 1910):

> Here, in short, was a male population in the prime of life, glowing with the virility of youth, and in the superb physical condition which a steady diet

of hard work produced. If they were not driven from the sheer animal exuberance to seek the female companionship of the brothels, they would have been driven to by the stinking atmosphere of their overcrowded rooming house.[2]

Imbalanced gender ratios go far in explaining the prevalence of prostitution in such places, but they do not tell the whole story.

"The oldest profession," has not been a static aspect of the human condition; many forces have affected the trade at different points in time. Historians argue that rapid industrialisation and urbanisation in the latter part of the nineteenth century led to an increase in the number of prostitutes. The family economy was crumbling and some single women who were faced with either unemployment or low wages as industrial workers or domestic servants opted for prostitution.[3] Simultaneously, sex and leisure were becoming increasingly commercialised. The men who migrated from rural areas could enjoy their anonymity in cities with expanded markets for sexual services.[4]

Meanwhile, the boom in natural resource extraction attracted large groups of single men to logging and mining camps on the northern and western frontiers. Those who travelled to and between these districts not only lived outside the confines of the family, but were citizens of rowdy towns that lacked (at least initially) a framework for regulating male sexual morality and leisure.[5] This was exactly why the Salvation Army was worried about the Yukon gold rush. "We must go after them!" it cried in 1898. "Men are rushing to the Klondike in the thousands, to the frozen regions of the North in search of wealth—sacrificing homes, wives, children and friends; risking…many subtle and deadly diseases and untold dangers by day and by night."[6]

The influx of men helped to establish Dawson as the most commercialized resource-based town in Canada at the time. As the service centre of the Klondike mining region, it provided laundry, banking, post offices, mining and outfitting supplies, and, last but not least, the notorious distractions offered by the dance-halls, theatres, saloons, and brothels. Not all men who frequented these establishments went in search of sex, of course. Many may simply have desired the company of women, and dance-halls, theatres, and saloons were the most obvious places to find them.[7]

The dance-hall owners regarded their role not as selling drunkenness or vice, but as offering "the common man" a place to relax far from the comforts of home. Or at least that is how they phrased it in a 1907 letter to the Minister of Justice. "Pleasures are few here," the group petitioned, and the dance-halls are "the only places of recreation in a country cut off from the rest of the world." Closing the dance-halls "means nothing to those who form the society life of Dawson...but to those who are beyond the pale of social recognition, though as honest and God fearing, the closing of these places would mean relegation to their lonely cabins."[8]

Dance-hall proprietors were on the defensive as late as 1907, but in the years closer to the whirl of the rush, loosened sexual mores were a likely symptom of the exuberant atmosphere. "No idle orders emanate from the police department of the Dominion government," it was announced in 1901, and so all unmarried couples who were living together were told to "either sacrifice themselves on the altar of conventionality by having the marriage ceremony performed or answer to the law which forbids the leading of such a life."[9]

Certainly not all single men who sought out sex had to pay for it. Some men pursued women for sexual trysts. Joseph Anderson, a steamship waiter from Seattle, testified at the trial of May Fields that he had neither given Fields money nor had sex with her: "I went out the same as any man would go out. I went to see the girl to see what I could get. To get intercourse if I could get it."[10] For some men, others of the same sex may have been the objects of their desire.[11]

About the men who did visit prostitutes in the Klondike, very little is known. While prostitutes' names were frequently listed in the newspapers, the same cannot be said for the clients. Most men (when given a choice) shied away from advertising their interactions with prostitutes. When the NWMP tried to convict Margaret Benoit for prostitution-related charges in April 1903, they subpoenaed three men who had been seen entering her cabin near the alley behind the Central Hotel at different times during the night. The testimony of these unnamed men, however, was evasive and they were evidently unwilling to testify against Benoit.[12] Possibly these were loyal customers who did not want to see Benoit punished; more likely they wanted to avoid incriminating themselves.

The only time male clients were named was in cases of robbery or when they were involved in direct conflicts with prostitutes that attracted the police. For the men who decided to press charges of theft against prostitutes, the loss of money outweighed any public embarrassment that resulted from a complaint to the police. In October 1899, Armen Legult came to town from the creeks, bringing with him the result of four months' work—$300 in gold dust. "After imbibing rather freely," he visited Fourth Avenue and, according to his story, "was enticed into a house of ill-fame conducted by Gussie Bulin, a colored woman." Legult claimed that his pocket was cut from his trousers and the sack containing the $300 in gold dust was taken from him by Gussie Bulin. Maintaining her innocence, Bulin swore that Legult had never entered her house until accompanied by a policeman. For lack of sufficient evidence, the magistrate discharged her, and she was free to ply her trade again.[13]

When Edward Cairns arrived at the Gold Hill Hotel, he made a point of presenting Maggie Richardson (a prostitute whom he had met on the road from Dawson to Grand Forks) as his wife to the proprietor and bartender. Later that night, he was allegedly robbed of $110 worth of gold dust by Maggie Richardson and her friend Maud

Westwood, but spent much time deliberating over whether to lay charges. Cairns admitted to the owner of the Gold Hill that he "would not take one thousand dollars to have his name appear in the Papers."[14]

The majority of alleged victims of theft probably shied away from the publicity. "Men have complained of having been 'rolled' on the Dance Hall premises, but are seldom, if ever, willing to prosecute," noted Z.T. Wood, commander of the Royal North-West Mounted Police (RNWMP). For men who were not as concerned about their moral standing, making accusations of theft—even false ones—carried little risk. After a night of drinking and carousing with Irene Howard and Neal Buckley—two dance-hall girls from the Orpheum—S.D. Freeman claimed he was missing two $1,000 dollar bills. Freeman reported to the police that while he was sleeping with Neal Buckley, Irene Howard rummaged through his clothes and stole the bills. A detective investigated the case, but was guaranteed by the manager of the Bank of British North America that Freeman would have had to go through the manager to get those bills. The manager had no record of the transaction.[15]

Prosecuting a dance-hall woman could be difficult because a large amount of money spent at a dance-hall could be easily accounted for. "They forget how much they spend and when they sober up all they know is...what cash they had, that they were drinking with a certain woman and are now broke," Sergeant McMillan explained. "On enquiry at the Dance Halls the...woman concerned and the bartender have a plausible story ready—beer costs $5.00 a bottle and wine $10 in boxes or rooms."[16] The proprietors, therefore, had to defend the reputation of their establishments. A group of dance-hall owners assured the federal minister of Justice that the men complaining of being robbed usually had "more imagination than money."[17]

Edith Green was one prostitute who did not appreciate being called a thief. In March 1901, Ted Erickson noticed that he was missing a pouch of $100 in gold nuggets from his pants pocket just as he was about to pay the bill at a restaurant. First he exclaimed "Ae tank Ae been robbed!" and then he returned "to whence he had but recently came"—the abode of Edith Green, "a large framed, rawboned female" from Fourth Avenue. When Erickson asked her to return his money, Edith allegedly proceeded to "turn herself loose in true pugilistic style, landing heavily with her right on Erickson's nose displacing a hunk of skin, then with an uppercut she caught him with her left on the mouth." Eventually, Constable Ferguson arrived on the scene, "declaring Edith the winner" before delivering "this typical Amazon" to jail.[18]

Occasionally, men were charged with infractions against prostitutes. In July 1899, James Brownley "demanded access to the nest of soiled doves in the tenderloin district" and, upon being denied admittance, kicked the door in with his brogans. Brownley was fined $50 and was ordered to repair the door. The "nest of soiled doves"—Blanche Montiguym, Trilby Dubois, Lillie Dubois, Vie Donangue, Jennie Benoit, Marguerite William and Alice Miller—was fined $50 and costs after this fiasco. The women were not fined for engaging in prostitution, but for ignoring a recent order from the NWMP to move to the official "Whitechapel" on Fourth Avenue that was set aside for their purposes.[19]

In a more violent incident in Klondike City in 1902, nineteen-year-old Fred Lachance struck Susanne Degreet on the head and forearm with a stick when she threw him out of her house. During this "rowdy state of affairs," Flora Navelle tried to help her friend Degreet, but ended up receiving a blow to the head that forced the lens of her glasses to fall out and caused her to bleed from the mouth. In police court, Magistrate Starnes sentenced Lachance to fifteen days of hard labour and told him that "a man was a coward who struck a woman." Twenty-six-year-old Belgian-born Susanne Degreet did not escape penalty either. She was given eight days of hard labour for being an inmate of a house of ill fame. The magistrate scolded that "if the girls [in Klondike City] could not behave themselves they would have to take the consequences."[20]

In a rather humorous case, two men were charged with stealing jewellery from three French prostitutes who were also en route to Dawson from Skagway, Alaska. While on a stopover in Whitehorse, R.E. West, Dawson news agent, and Ernest Levin, proprietor of the Arctic restaurant, decided to call on the women in their rooms at the White Horse Hotel. The crowd got "gloriously drunk," and some practical jokes ensued. When the women left West and Levin alone in the room for a moment, the men threw the women's suitcase into an open window of the Hotel Grand next door. Little did West and Levin know that the suitcases contained valuable jewellery. They maintained that it was not their intention to steal jewellery, but to use the clothes to pull an innocent prank: they planned to dress up in the women's clothes and return to the White Horse and surprise the crowd. Levin and West were charged with theft and were sentenced to one month and three months' imprisonment, respectively. In view of a petition he received and the "previous good character of the prisoners," the judge agreed to make the sentence as light as possible.[21]

A man's air of respectability, it seems, was an important factor when interactions with prostitutes brought him before the law. During a raid of the Fourth Avenue Hotel in 1908, a Mr. Richardson (no first name recorded) was found in the arms of Louise Misse, a prostitute. Richardson was called as a witness at Misse's trial, and he testified that he was not paying Misse for sex at all, but was offering her money as an incentive for Misse to find another calling. Richardson further assured Judge Craig that he had every ambition of marrying Louise Misse. Judge Craig was satisfied with Richardson's chivalrous intentions: "I have no reason to doubt Richardson's word...when a man, apparently respectable, says that he has paid a girl money to leave her life of prostitution and get other employment...one must have some respect for his evidence."[22]

It was a rare occasion when male callers as a group were the objects of serious complaint. Once, however, during the campaign to "clean up" South Dawson in 1902, its respectable citizens protested: "Drunk loafers seeking the companionship of that class of cattle knock at the first door they come to, rap on the windows, peep through open doors and otherwise make themselves so obnoxious that life under such conditions has about reached the limits of endurance."[23]

Men's activities could be subject to public scrutiny, but the extent of this was dependent on notions of class and respectability. Unless customers were particularly boisterous or went public with allegations of theft, they faded into the background as the unspoken feature of prostitution. Men benefited from the privilege of discretion in a way that these very public women did not. Occasional remarks of disapproval were hardly equal to the regulatory measures that prostitutes—or pimps for that matter—were subject to.

"The Class Of Men Who Neither Toil Nor Spin"[1]

The pallid pimp of the dead-line, the enervate of
the pen, One by one I weeded them out, for what
I sought was—Men.
—Robert Service, "The Law of the Yukon"

Lucy Miller and Emil Tomasson had known each other for
two years when Tomasson was arrested for living off the
avails of prostitution in 1899. The two had met in New
York, and had travelled to Seattle, Washington and Juneau,
Alaska before arriving in the Klondike. During this time,
Miller engaged in prostitution while Tomasson—who was
said to wear fine linen and have the jingle of gold in his
pockets—extracted her earnings.[2] At police court, Miller
testified that she was earning $10 to $20 per night, all of
which she was forced to hand over to Tomasson. Miller
further revealed that Tomasson had repeatedly beaten her
and otherwise treated her cruelly.[3]

This exploitative type of relationship between prostitute
and pimp may not have been uncommon in the Klondike,
but the pimps, known as "macques," were rarely portrayed
in such a predatory light. Rather than being considered
evil procurers, the macques were usually depicted as idle
and effeminate men who had never worked "honestly."
Unlike the hard-working miners who laboured on the
creeks, the macques allegedly spurned physical labour. Even

worse, they were financially supported by women.

The activities of the women who were prostitutes may have been tolerated at the height of the gold rush, but the men who lived off the avails of prostitution were the targets of police harassment and public scorn. Remarkably, however, the "respectable" men of Dawson who profited from the trade seem to have escaped scrutiny altogether.

On a cold night in November 1899, the police occasioned "quite a flutter among the soiled doves of the tenderloin district," when they awakened the residents of the various cribs. "With dishevelled hair and bleared eyes," the women opened their respective doors expecting to greet a belated caller. The purpose of this raid, however, was not to disturb the women, but to arrest the men known as macques in the "lower circles" of society. When tried by Major Perry, two of the five men arrested insisted that they were employed as cooks by certain denizens of the district. Although one of the men established a convincing defence, the other "evinced lamentable ignorance of the culinary art" and was sentenced to thirty days of hard labour, with no option of a fine.[4]

The ridicule of the macques in the pages of the *Klondike Nugget* was obviously a source of humour for readers. A sentence to hard labour at the NWMP woodpile was deemed an appropriate and comical punishment for men like Samuel Comfort who were "not familiar with toil":

> Samuel Dis-Comfort will be his name for the next four months.... It was a sad day for Samuel yesterday when, instead of getting off in police court with a fine, he was sentenced to four months on the royal fuel reduction works [the woodpile]...four months of discomfort for Mr. Comfort.... Samuel, you're up against the real thing now.[5]

A similar message was sent to Felix Duplau, who was charged with living off the avails of prostitution. "Six Months for Duplau—Living From Prostitution is no Picnic

When It Leads to the End of a Royal Saw," the headline read. Forty-one-year-old Duplau had been in the French army for several years. Physical labour was probably not foreign to him, though his five foot three inch, 175-pound frame may have suggested otherwise.[6]

Enoch Emmons (alias "Tony"), also sentenced to hard labour, was twice referred to in the jail record as being "very effeminate in his ways."[7] Effeminacy seems to have complemented the depiction of macques as indolent men unaccustomed to physical work. Those living off the avails were frequently described by the NWMP as being "pale in complexion" and having "delicate hands." Cryptic police-court columns were expected to be understood by the general public: "H. Williamson has soft, white hands, but works regular hours. $50 and costs solves the conundrum."[8]

The belief that the macques were financially supported by women contributed to their unmanly image. After Sigwold Rosafield Paulson was arrested for drunkenness in 1903, his mode of life was investigated and the laying of a more serious charge was the result. "Being of a systematic turn of mind," Addie Mantell of Klondike City had kept a cash book and ledger on which Paulson's name appeared "very often among the items of expense and outlay." It seems that the two were partners in both the business and the romantic sense, as one of the pages of Mantell's ledger read: "Sigwold Rosafield Paulson is my darling sweet shuger lump and preshes darling since 1901...the life time long I trust to be friends and tru companions and thank god if such be granted to addie mantell." She testified that since February 1901 she had transferred over $2,000 to Paulson. In passing his sentence, the judge was "very vigorous and scathing in his denunciation of men who live as Paulson had proven to live." It was noted that Paulson was "a pale, thin man of perhaps 30 years and, like all others who live as he is alleged to live, wears good clothes and has the air of a man not familiar with toil."[9]

When John Robert (a man with "delicate hands" who "frequently weeps when troubled," according to the

NWMP) was hauled off to jail on the charge of living off the avails of prostitution, the inmates of the infamous Bartlett House came to his rescue. The "madame," Lucille Martin, supplied Robert (who sported a blond moustache curled upwards) with a necktie and handkerchief for his appearance in police court. Meanwhile, inmates Marcelle Martin and Louise Coragaud blew kisses and displayed "other manifestations of affection." After his conviction, these women even went so far as to auction off all the contents of the house to raise the $3,000 bail money for John Robert. Their fundraising efforts liberated the man from six months of hard labour at the woodpile.[10]

The residents of the Bartlett House knew each other before their arrival in Dawson. They travelled over ice and snow together (along with Felix Duplau, another prosecuted pimp) in the winter of 1902.[11] It is *possible* that Robert's relationship may have been more friendly than parasitic. To this day the presumption of pimping under the Criminal Code is particularly strong where a man lives with a prostitute, as John Robert did. Unfortunately, however, there are only the very subjective *Nugget* reports to rely on for answers, and the paper banned publication of much of the evidence in the notorious Bartlett House case "owing to its nature which was most revolting."[12] The internal workings of the Bartlett House—particularly the role of John Robert—will forever remain concealed behind its peepholes and false door panels.

The reported stories about the macques served as lessons in appropriate standards of masculinity, but they also diverted attention away from the broader economic and social realities of prostitution.[13] "Why is the [pimp] more criminal or a greater menace to society than the owners of department stores and factories, who grow fat on the sweat of their victims, only to drive them onto the streets?"[14] asked Emma Goldman, an American anarchist of the early twentieth century. Pimps were not the only men who profited from the oldest profession. In the Klondike, as elsewhere, the targeting of macques obscured the fact that for businessmen, commercial interests put a more respectable face on their earnings from vice and spared them from the woodpile.

Prominent Pimps

> The poor unfortunates pay heavy rentals to a socialist—one DeLeon—who I fear represents more prominent men in the City. The situation has been chosen not by the women themselves or their managers ... but by speculators in Dawson who do not hesitate to make fortunes out of this particular class of crime.
> —Yukon Crown Prosecutor F.C. Wade to the federal Department of Justice

During his trip to Toronto in 1901, F.C. Wade wrote a letter from the National Club on Bay Street, alerting the federal Deputy Minister of Justice to "an organized sodom in the teeth of the women and children" of Dawson.[15] Rumour had it that when the NWMP ordered the prostitutes outside the town limits in 1901, "prominent men in the city" purchased options on lots in Klondike City and West Dawson, where many prostitutes were forced to relocate. "The vice is bad enough itself," decried Wade, "but that any group of supposed respectable people should organize themselves into a syndicate for the purpose of making money out of rentals obtained by such means is absolutely abhorrent."[16]

This was not the first mention of distinguished residents of Dawson seeking to profit from vice. There is evidence that three prominent citizens had purchased the half-acre lot and built the "cribs" in which the women were to live when they were forced to move from the business section on Front Street to the allotted tenderloin district on Fourth Avenue in 1899. Two real estate agents served as trustees who collected the $30-per-month rent for the owners. The landowners earned as much as $800 each in monthly rents.[17]

Such a system was not limited to the Klondike during this period. Although the names of elites were rarely found on tax assessment rolls of New York City, the tracing of multiple leases occasionally led to the families of the American establishment—the son of New York governor Hamilton Fish Jr., for example, and William Randolph Hearst, the publishing magnate and aspirant to political office.[18] As for the Yukon Crown prosecutor's specific accusations, the land registry shows that George DeLeon did indeed buy a series of adjacent lots in west Dawson.[19] As to whether he was the sole recipient of the rental earnings or whether, as F.C. Wade charged, DeLeon represented some fellow citizens, that is a matter for speculation.

Some prominent citizens' connection to the demimonde was less direct than land ownership. Wade had also complained about the firm of Stauf and Zilly and their role as agents for the financing of the "tenderloin district" on Fourth Avenue. Duff Pattullo (who eventually became premier of British Columbia) later joined Emil Stauf to form Stauf and Pattullo, after leaving his post as assistant gold commissioner in 1903. The new partnership—significant real estate, mining, insurance, and financial agents—had a range of clients, so it may be unfair to assume that the owners of brothel lands still ranked among them. It is certain, however, that they were agents for Ben Levy, owner of the Orpheum—the dance-hall that became the focus of May Fields' prostitution trial in 1908.

At the trial, manager John McCrimmon was called as a character witness for May Fields, a dance-hall girl who, like other employees of the Orpheum, was allegedly engaging in prostitution on the side. Crown Prosecutor James Pattullo (the brother of Duff Pattullo) became noticeably angry with McCrimmon's vague responses about his livelihood:

Q: Where have you been living—under a bushel basket?

A: No sir.

Q: And you have been mingling with these girls all along for the past two years and living off what they earn?

A: Not exactly.

Q: The only income you make is what these girls make for you—is that not right?

A: Yes sir, I have expenses to pay, the same as anyone.[20]

James Pattullo could hardly have been surprised by the testimonies he heard at the trial. In the previous year he had investigated the connection between prostitution and the dance-halls at the request of the federal Minister of Justice. The irony of the situation was that despite James Pattullo's awareness of his brother's business with the dance-hall, it was McCrimmon—the more direct actor—who was the focus of his hostility.

Many respectable businessmen who were not directly profiting from the dance-halls at least recognized that these establishments were a stimulant to the Dawson economy. Minister of the Interior Clifford Sifton's announcement in July 1901 that he would close the dance-halls was met with much resistance. NWMP commander Z.T. Wood pleaded that closing the dance-halls would wreak economic hardship, since it would put 200 people out of work in the middle of winter.[21] William Ogilvie, the commissioner at the time, reminded Sifton that the dance-hall owners had invested large sums of money and had been assured that they would not be interfered with without due notice being given.[22]

Sifton cancelled the order to close the dance-halls in 1901 after succumbing to public pressure. He may also have recognized the importance of liquor revenues to his government. Leading up to the federal election of 1901, regular Liberal party funds were supplemented by granting liquor permits in the Yukon. Liquor licenses were allegedly issued in exchange for contributions of one dollar per gallon to the Liberal party.[23]

Liquor licenses were more than a source of revenue. The regulations attached to licenses also acted as a mechanism to control prostitution in the post-rush period. In July 1902, the business community petitioned against new amendments to the Liquor License Ordinance Act. One amendment (in place between 1902 and 1904, and after 1907) put an end to the licensing of dance-halls and even prohibited any connection between a saloon and a dance-hall. Another amendment authorized the chief license inspector to cancel a liquor license if any part of a licensed hotel or saloon was being used for an "improper or immoral purpose" or if "any female suspected of being a prostitute" was found in the establishment. It was very obvious that these amendments were directed at eliminating prostitution in connection with dance-halls, yet included among the petitioners against them were such reputable firms as the Northern Commercial Company, White Pass and Yukon Route, Palmer Brothers, and the Ladue Company. The group argued that the enforcement of the new laws would "work great hardship upon not alone those who are engaged in that line of business, but upon many others doing business in the City of Dawson."[24]

To return to the letter from Yukon Crown Prosecutor F.C. Wade: was eradicating prostitution truly his goal, or was there a political motive in maligning the "Hungarian socialist" DeLeon, who had neither a Hungarian name nor a proven socialist bent?[25] The latter explanation seems more plausible. Around the time that Wade made his complaints to the Department of Justice, Dawson residents were debating the issue of incorporation, which would bring with it an elected instead of an appointed city council. Wade had vehemently opposed elected positions at the territorial level, as well as demands for incorporation from the Citizens' Committee. DeLeon, on the other hand, was a publicly recognized incorporation supporter and businessman who contributed $700 per year in taxes.[26]

Another likely motive of Wade's was that he wanted to

impress his superiors in Ottawa by expressing his disapproval of the official tolerance of prostitution in the Klondike. As the next chapter reveals, Prime Minister Laurier himself was under political pressure to stamp out vice in the Yukon. Finally, Wade was known to be generally bitter after he was passed over for a promotion to commissioner of the territory, and after he had been the subject of many complaints regarding his "incompatible positions" as Crown prosecutor, Clerk of the Court, and private counsel for several Dawson firms.[27]

Wade's letter stands as testimony to the intense politicization of prostitution—not only as a "moral" issue, but as a highly commercial one as well. As the next chapter amplifies, others like Wade realized the kind of political leverage that prostitution could provide, and made use of the issue accordingly.

CHAPTER 5

"From Pillar to Post and Back Again":
The Phases of Regulating Prostitution, 1898-1908

Transplantation and Toleration: 1898-1900

As the town of Dawson sprang up, newspapers around the world filled their pages with elaborate descriptions of the Klondike boom town. Dawson had surpassed all other North American mining camps, declared the *San Francisco Examiner:*

> Dawson is gold, whisky, and women in a riotous whirl. Not Leadville in vermilion heyday, nor Tombstone with the lid off, nor San Francisco in the flush of '49, had more picturesqueness than this camp has today.[1]

The more ambitious accounts (such as that of *Le Temps* of Paris) heralded a northern metropolis reaching international fame: "La nouvelle cité a pris la nocturne de Paris, la croissance spontanée et la fébrile activitée de Chicago. Cosmopolite autant que Rome."[2]

Although Dawson may have had a metropolitan air to it in 1898, it was still a frontier mining town with cramped conditions and limited goods and services. In the early days, "family values" had little clout, and the NWMP had more immediate concerns than morality and vice as thousands of people flooded into the region. Consequently, "immorality" was more visible—a fact that has not escaped the notice of many writers and commentators. In his Dawson-situated novel *The Spoilers* (1906), author Rex Beach explains, "The vices of a city, however horrible, are at least draped scantily by the mantle of convention, but in a great mining-camp they stand naked and without concealment."[3]

Mary Lee Davis' book *Sourdough Gold* (1933) presents a similar picture:

> No facet of that myriad-cut life flashed more flauntingly in the public eye. A scarlet coat might serve the embodied Law, but scarlet women were the most notable accents of Dawson's sights and bright lights. A blind man could have sensed their common presence and their influence.... In a wide open town such as Dawson boasted itself, no man or woman or child but some time, in some way, must come in contact with "the oldest profession."[4]

This account may be an embellishment, but its tone emerges from the permissive approach to regulating prostitution in Dawson at the onset of the rush. From 1898 to about 1900, prostitution was tolerated and supervised rather than suppressed. This is apparent from the official measures employed: fining, inspecting the women for venereal disease, and, by 1899, designating an area of town for the prostitutes' "cribs."

These measures reflected the notion that prostitution was a natural and necessary aspect of a mining community such as Dawson in which eighty percent of the men were single. This phase of regulation also represents the consolidation of commercial interests in Dawson City. Other places of business resented the prostitutes' occupation of what were considered to be "the choicest of city lots." The NWMP order in April 1899 for the women to move a few blocks away from the main commercial district had a financial, rather than a strictly moral, impetus.

In September of 1898, the police rounded up and fined 150 women, collecting $8,750 in the process.[5] The system of fining acted as a means of licensing prostitutes: the women paid their fines and then "smilingly departed from the temple of justice,"[6] free to ply their trade until the next round of penalties. The money raised from fining prostitutes went to a charitable cause—to the local board of health to pay for the care of the destitute sick at Dawson's two hospitals.[7] The practice of fining prostitutes, it seems, initially served as a source of revenue rather than a form of deterrence.

Mandatory medical inspections of women deemed to be prostitutes had the similar effect of licensing prostitutes and raising funds. The program was set up on the advice of Commissioner Ogilvie and NWMP superintendent Steele and was introduced to curtail the "deluge" of cases of men suffering from syphilis and other venereal diseases.[8] From October 1898 until January 1900, the territorial medical health officer and the assistant surgeon of the NWMP examined these women every two weeks at a cost of five dollars per visit.[9] At the outset, the income promised to be "a handsome one and the commission profitable," and the *Nugget* warned that the enforced regulation "should not be made a means of tremendous emolument to favourite doctors."[10] In return for their payment of five dollars, women free of venereal disease were given a letter certifying their health by the doctor. The procedure was not performed to protect the women who were examined, however, as there was no effective medical remedy for venereal disease until the 1930s.[11] The only thing medical inspection could accomplish was to alert men to the women they should avoid.

This program was in accordance with others at the time that accepted the inevitability of prostitution, but sought to control and contain the consequence—sexually

53

transmitted diseases. In the 1860s, Britain introduced the Contagious Diseases Acts in an attempt to control the spread of venereal disease in garrison towns and ports. Women who were identified as "common prostitutes" were subjected to a medical examination every two weeks and, if found to be afflicted with a venereal disease, could be sent to a certified hospital for up to nine months.[12] A successful campaign led by a coalition of evangelicals, working-class men, and feminists led to the repeal of the legislation in 1883, though a system of medical inspection persisted in parts of continental Europe. Aside from brief stints in St. Louis and New York, similar attempts at state regulation in American cities during this period were defeated.[13]

The Contagious Diseases Acts were transported to British North America in 1865 for a five-year period. They were never officially enforced, but a few municipalities set up red-light districts and programs for medical inspection of the women, just as was done in Dawson."[14] Montreal, for example, took this "Parisian" approach to regulating prostitution, as did the coal-mining town of Nanaimo, B.C.[15] In Halifax, commanders of the army and navy tried to pass a "Nova Scotian equivalent" to the British Contagious Diseases Acts by declaring notorious houses and districts off limits.[16]

Regulated prostitution was anathema to the Women's Christian Temperance Union (WCTU). In 1898, there was a call for the resignation of Lady Somerset (vice-president at large of the World WCTU), when she announced her support for the medical inspection of prostitutes in British army camps in India.[17] At the Sixth Convention of the World WCTU that year, president Francis Willard accepted Somerset's apology, but other delegates at the convention reiterated their disapproval of such practices: "we are unalterably opposed to any system of license or regulation of the social evil, and...we make it our solemn protest against the legal, voluntary or compulsory examination of either men or women, where this is done in the interests of impure relations."[18] Dr. Amelia Yeomans, vice-president of the Dominion WCTU, condemned Somerset's re-election and implored the Canadian union to resign from the international body: "we reaffirm that the first plank in our platform is no compromise with sin."[19] As we will see, this was exactly the attitude of the WCTU upon hearing about the situation in Dawson.

The scarlet women of Dawson were subjected to medical inspection and the payment of occasional fines, but were otherwise free to practise their trade on Paradise Alley and Second Avenue. However, as more "respectable" businesses set up shop alongside the "maisons de joie," their proprietors objected to the "vulgar" advertising of the denizens of the demimonde. In booming Dawson, with its growing commercial importance, it was considered a "most discreditable thing to see glaring signs of 'Jennie and Babe' and wanton use of names or places of respectable business houses" to attract the attention of passersby to those houses of ill fame.[20] (Unfortunately, the newspapers were unwilling to print exactly what the signs said.)

Not only had the women misappropriated and "put to base uses" the names and titles of these establishments, but they were deemed to be unfair competition for neighbouring saloon and hotel owners. Complaints like the following ensued: "In rented cabins with no property seizable by the law but some bawdy tapestries and curtains, with a case of cheap goods secured from a friend on credit, these damsels enter into competition with the men who have expended vast sums of money."[21]

Despite the usual reluctance by saloon and hotel owners to be taxed, these men welcomed the Yukon Council's plans to draw up a Liquor License Ordinance that would require an annual licensing fee of $2,000. It was hoped that the licensing fee would create a financial barrier for "the denizens of Second Avenue and their ilk."[22] The Ordinance passed in 1899, but it was not only the hefty fee (that ended up being $1,000) that would have put these women out of business. Under the Liquor License ordinance, only saloons, hotels, and steamboats could be licensed. Further, hotels in the Yukon were required to have at least ten bedrooms, as well as a stable for six or more horses. Saloons had to be "a good, substantial building" with "a suitable privy and urinal, which shall at all times be clean."

The 1899 Ordinance was one way of discouraging the women from plying their trade on the main streets, and a NWMP order later the same year ensured their eviction. Superintendent Sam Steele commanded that since the area that the prostitutes occupied was "required for business purposes," the women would have to move to a section of town set aside for them. Respectable Dawson rejoiced: "No longer may the woman in scarlet occupy the choicest of city lots and flaunt her crimson colours on Dawson's crowded streets; no longer may the seductive window tap beguile the innocent prospector or hurrying man of business."[23]

The removal of the prostitutes from the growing commercial section of town was part of a battle for control of urban space. By the time the NWMP decree was to be enforced, the women of the demimonde were considered unpopular, if not hazardous, denizens of the district. After an enormous fire on April 26, 1899 destroyed 117 buildings and caused over $1 million in damage, a jury determined that the fire had started in dance-hall girl Helen Holden's room above the Bodega Saloon. It was surmised that the demimonde was "most conducive to fires" and the official recommendation was that "all women of the town" be excluded from public buildings other than licensed hotels.[24]

Though the command to relocate the demimonde was serious, the NWMP had no intention of actually putting an end to prostitution. "These girls seem to be in the eyes of the majority of the community a necessary evil," Superintendent Steele admitted.[25] The *Nugget* stressed that by being moved from Second Avenue to the assigned areas, the women were "not swept from the earth by an iron hand, but transplanted."[26] Indeed, the new designated area ensured that the women would remain a vibrant part of

Dawson, the system of medical inspection would inhibit the spread of venereal disease, and fining would serve as both a resource for the municipal treasury and a form of licensing. For the time being, the conditions in this frontier mining community seemed to justify a tolerance of prostitution that would probably be deemed unacceptable in most other cities in Canada. It should be no surprise that serious criticism from the forces of morality was just ahead on the horizon.

Northern Exposure: 1900-1901

In November 1899, Minister of the Interior Clifford Sifton was informed of the procedure by which the prostitutes were obtaining their health certificates. Sifton—who by this point faced allegations of corruption in his administration of the Yukon[27] and was anxious that "immorality" in Dawson not become an issue in the upcoming federal election—realized that the medical certificates could be construed as an official license to engage in prostitution. Consequently, he telegraphed Yukon Commissioner William Ogilvie, ordering that he command the police surgeon to terminate the issuing of these certificates of health.[28]

Sifton was surely pleased that he had covered his tracks. Six months later he had to respond appropriately to a letter from Mrs. Kate Heaman, head of the Social Purity Department of the London, Ontario WCTU concerning rumours of unchecked vice in Dawson. "From a conversation with a lady just returned from the district," together with "reliable information received from other sources," Mrs. Heaman was compelled to write to Sifton on behalf of the WCTU in June of 1900:

We have learned that there are many profligate women there, that are recognized by the authorities, who instead of arresting and punishing them, confine their residence to one portion of the town, which is known as the "lost woman's quarters" and that in the dance-halls, girls are paid commission on all drinks sold over the bar, and all night long induce men to drink.[29]

Sifton's deputy minister, James Smart, sent a confident reply. He stated that the only reference to prostitution that had been brought to the attention of the Minister related to the medical certificates that were issued to the women. Immediately upon being advised of this, Mrs. Heaman was assured, Sifton had ordered that the examinations and issuing of certificates cease. "Of course you will understand," Smart added, "that there may be difficulties of which neither the Minister nor yourself may know in connection with the suppression of vice in an out of the way mining camp like Dawson."[30]

The catalyst for cracking down on prostitution in Dawson City came from the "outside." By 1900, the iniquitous Klondike had captured the attention of southern moral reform organizations like the WCTU. The situation in Dawson spoke to the cardinal concerns of the WCTU. Not only was it opposed to official regulation of prostitution, but the rumours of vice in the Klondike fed into the notion that the Yukon, like other northern locales, was dangerously out of reach of the corrective arm of moral reform. The issue may also have provided a venue for the group to vent its anger toward the Laurier government. In 1898, Laurier ignored a majority vote in favour of prohibition (except in Quebec) in a plebiscite that the WCTU had campaigned for ardently.[31]

Possibly aware of these political undertones, the Department of the Interior immediately forwarded Mrs. Heaman's letter to Commissioner Ogilvie in the Yukon, expecting a response. Ogilvie, despite having already received a condensed version of the WCTU letter from William Muloch (member of parliament and secretary of the Dominion Temperance Alliance), declined to reply.

Clifford Sifton wrote a second letter to Ogilvie (who happened to be a relative of Mrs. Sifton), stating that he believed it was high time for Ogilvie to intervene: "it seems to me that a considerable increase in stringency is required. I see no reason why what is known as dance-halls but which are in reality, as I understand it, bar-rooms with women of ill-repute in attendance, should not be summarily suppressed."[32]

Ogilvie responded to the charges of his southern critics. "I recognize fully the good work done by the WCTU and which they are now attempting to do," he declared. Nonetheless, Ogilvie lamented "a great ignorance on the outside" as to the conditions in Dawson City.[33] In his reply to Sifton, he explained that toleration was the only realistic approach to an inevitable aspect of a frontier mining community:

> Dance-halls are an evil, which no one attempts to gainsay; but at the same time they are like many other evils, considered absolutely necessary under certain conditions.... As long as human nature is what it is, this evil will exist in some form or another, and no legislation can be enacted which will abolish it.[34]

In order to render these convictions palatable to his superiors in Ottawa, Commissioner Ogilvie expressed concern for the men and women who could be the victims of vice suppressed: "To abolish [the dance-halls] would be to throw a lot of women into a more vicious life, as many of these women would not resort to ordinary prostitution but would be leeches on the general mining public."[35]

The Department of the Interior was not impressed with Ogilvie's attitude, and the exchanges between Ottawa and Dawson became very heated. Deputy Minister Smart did not appreciate any intimation that either Sifton or he was part of "a great ignorance on the outside" about existing conditions in Dawson. An angry letter was forthcoming:

"Your suggestion that if these open places are suppressed…those gaining a livelihood in dance-halls will be driven to a more vicious life, could hardly, in this enlightened age, be such an argument as would appeal to the people of this country as a sufficient reason for permitting the evil to continue." Smart assured Ogilvie and Major Wood of the NWMP that they were both "labouring under a very erroneous impression as to what the Minister's wishes are in this relation."[36]

Ogilvie, though, hardly seemed ruffled by Ottawa's criticisms nor by the complaints from religious proponents of moral reform. He disregarded the WCTU's insistence that "so grave and shameful an evil" was a "disgrace to our Christian civilisation" and referred to those opposed to official regulation of prostitution as "extreme moralists and religious cranks."[37] Eventually Ogilvie bowed to authority and announced that the dance-halls were to close by March 15, 1901.

This did not signal the end of the Klondike dance-halls, however. Ottawa's deadline for the closures extended into the reign of Ogilvie's replacement as commissioner, James H. Ross. Like his predecessor, Ross also stood his ground against Sifton and (with the support of the Dawson business community) refused to put the order into effect.[38] In the years following, periodic threats to close the dance-halls were made but were never followed through on. Instead, the Liquor License Ordinance was altered a few times to suit the reigning moral majority of the day.

Ogilvie had resigned as commissioner in February 1901, citing health and other reasons, "some of which are personal dislike of many things in connection with my position."[39] Certainly one of these "things" was Minister Sifton, for there is no doubt that the antagonism between the two men hastened Ogilvie's resignation. The cause of the animosity was deeper than the dance-hall debates: the underlying issue seems to have been the territorial election of October 1900 and Ogilvie's desire for a more politically autonomous territorial government.

Ogilvie had presented many grievances on behalf of the citizens of Dawson to the Governor General, Lord Minto, when he visited the Yukon in August 1900. These prompted Minto to conclude that "in any country but this, public opinion of the Minister [Sifton] as expressed in ordinary conversation would be enough to ruin any man. My verdict is criminal administration by the Minister of the Interior."[40] Many of these complaints became territorial election issues, and Ogilvie sided with the two candidates who would be the first elected representatives on the Yukon Council. These men drummed up much public support by their opposition to the Laurier government's administration of the Yukon. Minister Sifton denied Conservative charges that Ogilvie had been fired, but there is evidence that the commissioner's job was made difficult for him after the territorial election.

Politics and morality are a potent mix. Ogilvie's defence of the dance-halls of Dawson symbolized a bitterness towards "outside" interference in territorial affairs. Sifton's accusations were attempts to deflect criticism of the Liberal government's administration of the Yukon, as well as efforts to maintain his integrity as a politician. Vice, it seems, could be manipulated to suit many purposes. Responses to "immorality" reflected colliding agendas and provided ammunition for disgruntled political actors such as the WCTU, William Ogilvie, James Smart, Clifford Sifton, and F.C. Wade, among many others.

At least the dance-halls stimulated Dawson's precarious economy, but flagrant prostitution in the designated area of town was becoming a bane to both property and family values. By late 1901, complaints escalated from residents about the "disreputable element" who lived between Fourth and Fifth Avenues, particularly after it was announced in November that a public school was to be built on Third Avenue. The officials were in a difficult position, however, since this area had been officially set aside for the prostitutes' use in 1899.

Wood issued orders that all music and noise was to

cease at midnight. Women were prohibited from appearing at windows or on the street, where they might be considered unsuitably dressed.[41] This was a superficial solution, however. As the protests continued, the Yukon Council decided to act, declaring that the women would be forced to vacate Fourth and Fifth Avenues as soon as the weather improved.[42] Regulating vice in the Klondike had to be tempered with consideration for the long, harsh winters, it seems. With spring's arrival, though, Major Wood ordered the women out of the town limits as of May 1, 1901. This sent most of the women to West Dawson (across the Yukon River via a ferry), Klondike City (across the Klondike River via a bridge), or out of the territory altogether.

Many of the women found that the longer commute to Dawson was adversely affecting their incomes and so began slipping back into town to ply their trade. In a letter to the editor in August 1901, a resident of Dawson (A.J.R.) complained that finding the city ordinance not enforced, the "painted bipeds" had returned and were infesting "every available nook and corner in the city." A.J.R. described an incident that a businessman had recently recounted to him:

> "I don't know where I should take my family if I brought them in; the other night (in one of the best hotels in the city) a man came stumbling up the stairs drunk and yelling 'I want a woman! I want a woman!' Immediately the lady (?) on duty was heard to say 'Keep still! Shut up your noise and I'll find you a woman'....This is a fine state of affairs to have in the very centre of the capital of the Yukon territory."[43]

Finally, this distressed Dawsonite griped: "The NWMP do nothing because no one kicks and the city council, when asked reply, 'well we have passed the ordinance, that's all we can do.'"[44]

By the spring of 1902, however, concerned citizens in the centre of the capital of the Yukon Territory had garnered more clout.

CHAPTER 6

The "Moral Flooding" of 1902: Cracking Down on Prostitution

The NWMP order to keep the prostitutes out of Dawson forced many women to try new tactics. Those who lived in West Dawson or Klondike City ventured into town during the evenings as streetwalkers. Others opened cigar stores and laundry places as fronts for houses of ill fame. Prostitution had previously been relegated to "the official Whitechapel," but it was now creeping into new areas of Dawson. As South Dawson became a favoured locale, its more respectable citizens waged a campaign against these "intruders" in 1902.

The police were called upon to make more arrests as the relative tolerance of prostitution was put on the back burner. The year 1902 marked an increase in women's conviction rates for prostitution-related charges. However, this campaign against prostitution was about more than filling the police court. It symbolized Dawson's shift from a mining camp to a town with a stable middle class intent on proving that Dawson was as refined as any southern city. But sin or no sin, Dawson was facing enormous economic uncertainty in the post-rush period. For "respectable" citizens, battling prostitution was part of the search for stability in the Klondike's uncertain future.

The stories of the "scarlet women" of Dawson—as told in the courtroom and reported in the newspapers—provided a venue by which ordinary Dawsonites could distinguish their own world from the demimonde. These reports, alluring to even the most respectable citizens, reveal a simultaneous fascination with and revulsion toward the women. In the *Nugget* columns, the police court was like a stage that could be "enlivened by the scent of patchouli and the giggles of gaily dressed women."[1]

When nine women brought with them "a great show of furs and the rustle of silks" to the police court, the dramatics of the courtroom seem to have been choreographed by the reporter:

> All the smiles vanished from their faces. The girls huddled together as if they were afraid they would fall down and faint. There were heavy sighs and the faces of all were blanched. There was a stillness in the court in which one might have heard ten pins drop, perhaps more.

> After Justice Macaulay had enjoyed the situation for a couple of minutes, he said, "I impose this punishment upon you now, but I am going to suspend sentence. If ever you are brought before me again, there will be no trial, but this sentence will immediately be put into effect. You may go now."

The writer concluded: "in an instant they had vanished like a bad dream, and the cold air was freshening up the atmosphere of the court room."[2]

The Klondike prostitutes could have quite an effect on air quality, it seems. This imagery of stale air was invoked again when their presence was discovered in the business district and residential area of South Dawson in the spring of 1902. Allegedly, the prostitutes brought with them "an atmosphere...reeking with a pollution so that the worst poison is mild in comparison."[3]

Significantly, the complaints emanating from South Dawson were among the first references to the ill effects of prostitution on "virtuous" women and children. A

Diamond Tooth Gertie's – Can-can dancers on stage, present day. The can-can girls are an important part of today's Klondike gold rush lore, but the truth is that they probably weren't on stage in Dawson until the late 1960s. (Yukon Archives)

ABOVE – The "scales"
at the summit of the
Chilkoot Pass was the
most gruelling part of
the Trail. The summit
has snow on it even in
mid-summer.
Stampeders were
required to carry a
considerable amount of
goods in order to avoid
the NWMP at Canada
customs.

RIGHT – Packers on
the Chilkoot Trail
c.1897. First Nations
men and women, like
the two (probably
Tlingit) people
pictured here, were
hired to carry gold
seekers' goods over the
Trail. The Chilkoot
Trial was an inland
trade route for the
coastal Tlingit for
thousands of years
prior to the gold rush.

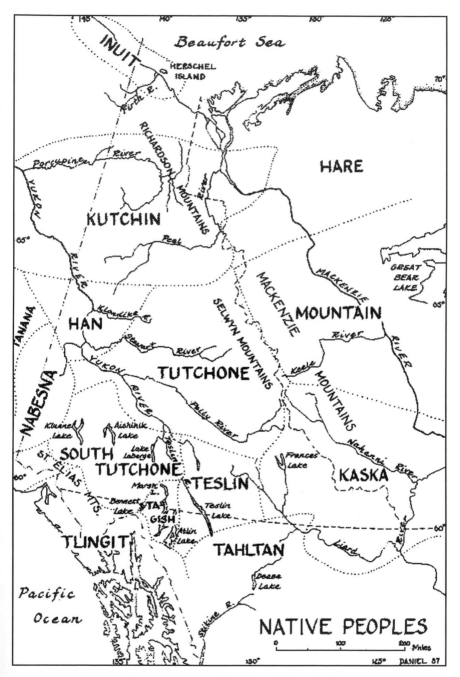

Aboriginal language groups of the Yukon. (Yukon Archives)

ABOVE – Panning for gold, 1897.

BELOW – Sluicing 12 Below Lower Dominion Creek, June 1903. As early as 1898, large consolidated mining companies began replacing gold panning with more efficient methods of extracting the alluvial gold.

ABOVE – Actresses crossing the Dyea River on the way to the Klondike via the Chilkoot Pass.

BELOW – "Loose" women of the Klondike were still the subject of intrigue
even decades after the rush. *American Weekly*, April 1943

ABOVE – Photo is entitled "A Group of Women Workers."
Larss & Duclos were professional photographers who, as visual chroniclers of the Klondike gold rush, staged many photos with prostitutes and dance-hall women.

BELOW – "The Pavilion" c.1898. Z.T. Wood, Commander of the NWMP, claimed that many dance-hall women lived above the Pavilion and the Criterion dance-halls in 1900.

"One of the Girls"—probably May Fields—of Dawson.

FREEDOM
WILL SHRIEK

At Police Barracks This Evening

When Former Inmates of Bartlett House Will Complete Sixty Day Sentences.

ABOVE – This *Klondike Nugget* article from July 1903 announces the release of the women of the infamous Bartlett House (Lucille and Marcelle Martin, and Louise Corragaud) from jail.

BELOW – Photo is entitled, "Goddesses of Liberty Enlightening Dawson, Y.T."

This evening after dinner, supper or whatever the evening meal at the police prison is called, has been served, the three French women, Lucille and Marcelle Martin and Louise Corragaud, who since May 12th have been busy in the laundry department of the prison and incidentally serving sixty days time for keeping and inhabiting a disorderly house, the Bartlett on Third avenue, will emerge into the Yukon ozone as free women, the terms of their sentences having been complied with and the washboards and smoothing irons with which they have been daily associated will know them no more.

The muscles which honest toil has implanted upon their ootsey tootsey arms will gradually depart like marks of fire from a singed cat. The blisters on their fingers from sticking them in their mouths and then touching them on the irons to see if they were sufficiently hot to impart the proper crease to convict pants will fade away like morning dew from a Mother Hubbard squash vine. The sunlight of heaven will kiss their golden tresses and the God-given zephyrs will renew the bloom on their prison-blanched cheeks. Truly the memory of this evening should long remain green in the thinkers of Lucille, Marcelle and Louise.

GODDESSES OF LIBERTY ENLIGHTING DAWSON, Y.T.

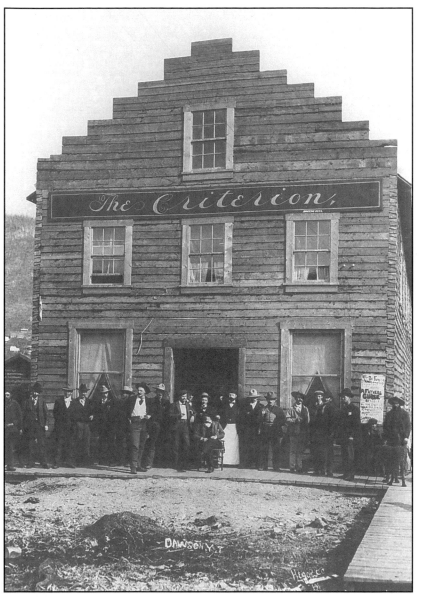

"The Criterion" c.1899.

KNOW ALL MEN BY THESE PRESENTS, that I John McCrimmon
of Dawson, in the Yukon Territory, Lessee of the Orpheum Dance
Hall do hereby agree to hire and employ the undersigned women
and girls as employees in my Dance Hall on the terms and conditions following:

I agree to pay to each and every of the undersigned
women and girls one half of all moneys earned by them in dancing
or selling refreshments in and about the Dance Hall. Each and
every of the said women and girls to receive checks for all
dances and refreshments sold and to be entitled to cash the
said checks at the Office of the Cashier in the Dance Hall
every night when the said Dance Hall closes. Each girl and
woman is to appear on the Dance Hall floor at the hour of 9
o'clock every evening and to remain there continuously with
the exception of such hours for meals as the Manager may decide
until the hour of 5 o'clock on the following morning and while
inside of the Dance Hall such woman and girl is to conduct
herself in an orderly and respectful manner. *Any woman or
girl is liable to dismissal at any time for breach or shame of
dance hall* No girl shall absent herself from the Dance Hall
between the hours of 9 o'clock P.M. and the hour of 5 o'clock
A.M. next morning without the consent from the Manager.

Dated at Dawson, in the Yukon Territory, this 4ᵗʰ day
of May, A.D. 1908.

J. H. McCrimmon

We the undersigned hereby agree to become employees
of the said John McCrimmon on the terms and conditions above
set forth and to perform our duties in the said Dance Hall to
the best of our ability and according to the said conditions.

Ray Hart
Bette Bartwell
Lucille
Lena Baylon
May Kinnier
Daisy McDonnell
Allie Jackson

Female employees of the Orpheum Theatre in 1908 had to sign this contract that
was designed to prevent those who were prostitutes from using the dance-hall as a
place to meet customers. "Lots of girls make appointments to go to eat with
different gentlemen," the manager explained. (Yukon Archives)

Vide Criminal Code
FORM FFF (Section 872.)

Warrant of Commitment upon a Conviction in the First Instance.

CANADA :
Yukon Territory }

To all or any of Peace Officers in the Yukon Territory, and to the Keeper of
the Royal North West Mounted Police Guard Room, at Dawson,
in the said Yukon Territory,

WHEREAS one MAY FIELDS,
late of Dawson, in the Yukon Territory,

was on **Saturday the 4th day of July, 1908,** *IN THE TERRITORIAL COURT OF THE YUKON TE*
convicted before the undersigned C. D. MACAULAY, *and the CRIMINAL JURISDICTION VESTED IN THE*
xxxxxxxxxxxx in and for the said Yukon Territory, *for that the* for that the said
May Fields, at Dawson, in the Yukon Territory, on the 1st day of
July, 1908, and on divers other times within the space of six
months previous thereto, was the keeper of a bawdy house situate
and being on 4th Avenue between York and Duke Streets, at said
Dawson; being thereby a loose, idle or disorderly person or
vagrant; Contrary to section 238, sub-section 'j', and
section 239 of the Criminal Code of Canada.

and it was thereby adjudged that the said **MAY FIELDS**
for **HER** offence should be imprisoned in the **Royal North West Mounted Police**
Guard Room *at* **Dawson,**
in the said Yukon Territory; *for the term of*
THREE MONTHS with Hard Labour; such term of imprisonment
to date from the 1st day of July, A.D., 1908;

These are therefore to command you, the said Peace Officers, or any one of
you, to take the said **MAY FIELDS** and
HER safely to convey to the said **Guard Room** *at* **Dawson,**
aforesaid ; and there to deliver **HER** to the said keeper thereof, together with this precept :
And I do hereby command you, the said keeper of the said **Guard Room**
to receive the said **MAY FIELDS**
into your custody in the said **Guard Room** , there to imprison **HER**
for the term of **THREE MONTHS with Hard Labour, to date, as**
aforesaid, from the said 1st day of July, A.D., 1908.

and for your so doing, this shall be your sufficient
warrant
Given under my hand and seal, this **4th** day of **July,**
in the year 190 **8** at **Dawson,** in the Yukon Territory aforesaid.

A JUDGE OF THE TERRITORIAL COURT OF THE YUKON TERRITORY
HAVING THE CRIMINAL JURISDICTION VESTED IN THE POLICE
MAGISTRATE FOR DAWSON.

May Fields was a dance-hall woman working at the Orpheum
when she was convicted of keeping her residence—the Fourth
Avenue Hotel—as a bawdy house. (Yukon Archives)

To The Honorable James H.Ross,

    and to the

        Members of the Yukon Council.

Sirs,-

        We the undersigned residents and rate-payers of the City of Dawson do most respectfully petition that the Ordinance recently passed by Your Honorable Body respecting the sale of intoxicating liquors, in so far as the same relates to theatres, concert and dance halls, be not enforced at the present time.

        In support of our petition we beg to submit that the enforcement of that portion of the Ordinance at the present time will work a great hardship upon not alone those who are engaged in that line of business, but upon many others doing business in the City of Dawson, including more especially the owners of buildings in which such theatres, dance and concert halls have heretofore been conducted; hotel keepers and merchants, many of whom have contracts with and have extended lines of credit to the proprietors and employees of such places, and who will sustain great loss if that portion of the Ordinance is immediately placed into force and effect.

        We most respectfully suggest that the portion of the Ordinance above referred to remain inoperative until on or about the first day of October next, thereby giving sufficient time for those interested to adjust the contracts and obligation in the premises.

        And Your Petitioners as in duty bound, will ever pray.

    Dated at Dawson, Y.T., this tenth day of July A.D.1902.

Name   Occupation

[signatures]

North American Trans. & Trad. Co.

ABOVE and ACROSS – Morality aside, the reality was that prostitution and dance-halls stimulated the Dawson economy. In 1902, fifty "respectable" businessmen signed this petition against changes to the Liquor License Ordinance aimed at curbing prostitution. (Yukon Archives)

ABOVE – It was at the Gold Hill Hotel in Grand Forks that Maggie Johnson and Maud Westwood allegedly stole $110 in gold dust from Edward Cairns in 1903.

ABOVE – Front Street with a view of the Orpheum Theatre c.1900.

SIGN A BLIND.

Dora Walls Held to Answer on a Serious Charge.

Dora Wells whose sign on her house on Second avenue reads 'San Francisco Laundry,'' was before the police court this morning on the charge of being the proprietor of a rough, bawdy and disorderly house. She pleaded not guilty and was remanded until next Tuesday when the case will be tried.

Dora is said to be the wife of Frank Salas now doing six months for living from the avails of vice, his enamorata being a resident of Klondike city.

The police say they have strong evidence against the Wells woman who is alleged to use the laundry sign only as a blind.

LEFT – Some prostitutes used "legitimate" business signs such as those of a laundry, dressmaker, or cigar store, to disguise what was, in many cases, a bawdy house. Dora Wells was convicted, and it was said that she appeared in court "looking as though her bicycle pathway through life was strewn with carpet tacks." (*Klondike Nugget*, 22 May 1903.)

ABOVE – First stores in Dawson, 1898.
The huge influx of people even sustained a market for oysters.

BELOW – Front Street. Business flourished
as the stampeders purchased supplies and services.

ABOVE – The "Whitechapel" of Dawson where the prostitutes "cribs" were located. Between 1898–1901, the trade was tolerated by local officials.

BELOW – Women believed to be prostitutes peering out of their "cribs."

The W.C.T.U.

Rooms, 240 Dundas Street,

London, Ont., June, 27th, 1900.

Hon Clifford Sifton,

Dear Sir,

I have been instructed by the W.C.T.U. of this city to call your attention to facts that exist in the Yukon District, in Dawson City.

We have learned that there are many profligate women there, that are recognized by the authorities, who instead of arresting and punishing them, confine their residence to one portion of the town, which is known as the "lost woman's quarters" and that in the Dance Halls, girls are paid commission on all drinks sold over the bar, and all night long induce men to drink. We have long heard these facts hinted at, but when they were constantly denied we have hoped they might not be true, but from a conversation with a lady just returned from that district, together with reliable information received from other sources, we find that the stories are only too true.

In the interest of our "Social Purity Dept" we implore you as Minister of the Interior that you would do all in your power, both by personal influence and vote, to suppress so grave and shameful an evil, that is a disgrace to our Christian civilization.

This matter is of deep interest to us all, because as many boys from all parts of Canada are in the mining regions, and make Dawson their permanent or temporary headquarters. For the sake of our Motherhood, for the sake of our wifehood, for the sake of our boyhood, we pray you to act speedily in this matter. Trusting to hear soon of this evil being abolished.

Yours on behalf of the Union, Mrs.Kate Heaman,
Cor. Sec. 461 York St., London,Ont.

Letter from the London, Ontario Women's Christian Temperance Union (WCTU) to the Minister of the Interior, alerting him to the presence of "profligate" women in Dawson. (Yukon Archives)

An Idle Rumor.

It has been reported around town for the past two days that the police have issued a second order to the demi-monde to the effect that they must again move, this time from Klondike City. The rumor is wholly without foundation as it is not the intention of the police or Yukon council to further molest these women except in csaes of disorder and flagrant infractions of the law. So long as they choose to live quietly in Klondike City they are at liberty to do so. It is said, however, that the women who moved to Klondike City are not satisfied with their location and feel that they are very much sidetracked and in consequence many of them will relocate in West Dawson. But why the latter place should be considered more frequented than Klondike City is not apparent. It is believed that the handicap which the original order placed upon these women will result in the greater part of them eventually leaving the vicinity of Dawson entirely, also of the district.

ABOVE – Klondike City was situated across the Klondike River via the Ogilvie bridge. "Lousetown," as it was also known, was at the convergence of the Klondike and Yukon rivers.

LEFT – After the NMWP ordered the women out of the town limits in May 1901, many relocated to the suburbs of Klondike City and West Dawson, or they left the territory altogether. (*Klondike Nugget*, 3 May 1901.)

Some women cigar store owners used their business
as a front for a bawdy house.

CRUSADE HAS BEGUN

To Keep Dissolute Wo-men Within Doors

Two Klondike City Females Visit City Last Night and Are Jailed

The police say there was a notic-able scarcity of dissolute women on the streets last night, the warning published in the Nugget of yesterday having served to keep them within doors.

The names of Polly Berge and Mar-got Benoit who reside in Klondike City do not appear on the Nugget's circulation list and as a consequence they remained in blissful ignorance of the decree against women of their stamp roaming the streets at night. The result was that, arrayed in gorgeous splendor, they came over to Dawson during the night but they only returned as far as the barracks, having been arrested and escorted to that district receptacle by the police.

The two women were not ready for trial this morning and were remand-ed to jail until 2 o'clock this after-noon. They secured the services of an attorney, but their line of de-fence was not made known at this morning's session.

This is the beginning of a crusade started for the purpose of keeping dissolute women off the street and there is little doubt but that it will be found very effective.

LEFT – Pauline Berge and Margaret Benoit were convicted during the "crusade" to clean up Dawson in 1902. The two later made a successful appeal to the Territorial Court, where Judge Craig held that so long as prostitutes were not accosting men, they had "the same rights on the streets as anybody else." (*Klondike Nugget*, 21 August 1902.)

RIGHT – John Robert, the macque of the Bartlett House, is convicted for living off the avails of prostitution. (*Klondike Nugget*, 12 May 1903.)

SIX MONTHS FOR ROBERT

Must Perform Hard La-bor During Period

Convicted and Sentenced for Liv-ing from Avails of Pros-titution.

John Robert was this morning sen-tenced in police court by Mr. Justice Macaulay to six months at hard la-bor in the penitentiary and to pay a fine of $50. In default of the pay-ment of the fine three additional months at hard labor are added to the sentence.

The hearing of evidence in Robert's case was concluded yesterday after-noon but owing to its nature which was most revolting its publication is precluded. Lucille Martin was re-called to the witness stand this morning to answer the question as to when she left Paris, Robert having sworn that he left there in December of 1901. At first the woman said she could not remember but being pressed for answer said she left Paris for America about the middle of Oc-tober, 1901.

Attorney Aikman for the accused spoke 40 minutes. He reviewed the evidence of all the witnesses, going closely into that of the police and his client. He closed with a strong plea for dismissal of the charge.

Crown Prosecutor Pattullo spoke only 20 minutes but in that short time he showed where the crown had made a strong case, where, in fact, the accused had convicted himself out of his own mouth.

His lordship carefully reviewed much of the evidence, commenting at length on the loathsomeness of the character of much of it. He said when the statute providing for the punishment on such charges was pass-ed he had no idea that the lawmakers at Ottawa knew of the degradation implied in the term "living from the avails of prostitution" and he fur-ther said that he intends, in com-pliance with his duty as a judge, to write the department at Ottawa ad-vising that the law in the statutes of the state of Washington providing punishment for the class known as macques be substituted for the pre-sent Canadian law. His lordship then passed sentence as before noted.

Attorney Aikman gave notice of appeal from the decision and sen-tence. The court interposed no objec-tion and fixed the amount of bail pending an appeal at $1500 cash, or Robert's personal bond of $3000 and two sureties in the sum of $1500 each.

ABOVE – The new Court House, 1901.

BELOW – NWMP Officer's Mess, Dawson, 1900.
Back Row: T.A. Wroughton, W. Thompson, D. Howard,
R.P. McLennan, L. Crosby, Dick Cowan, W. Routledge
Front Row: Judge Craig, C. Starnes, Z.T. Wood,
A.E. MacDonnell, E.C. Sinclair

In 1902, there was a crusade not only to keep prostitutes out of the territory, but Asian people as well. (*Klondike Nugget*, 10 July 1902.)

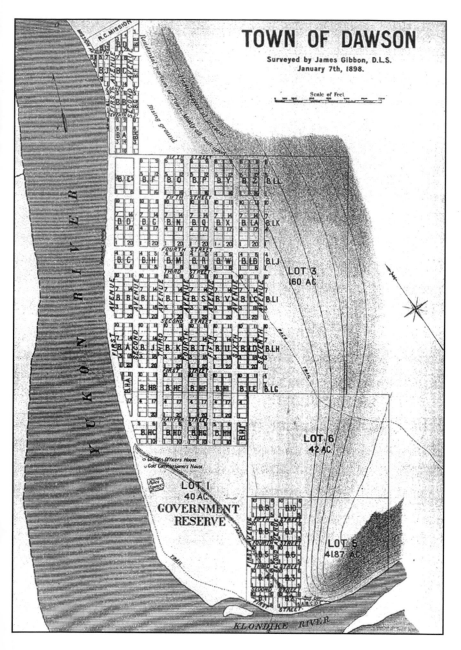

Survey of Dawson, 1898. (Yukon Archives)

DAILY KLONDIKE NUGG

DAWSON, Y. T. FRIDAY FEBRUARY 14, 1902.

CENTS ABROAD

Are Robbed of Their
In Seattle and San
Francisco.

DREWS WAS VISITED

Donald Brutally Beat-
By Footpads

ALL OF HIS MONEY

of Henry Bray's Famliy
Seattle—Klondikers
r Spending Mo ey.

Richard McAndrews
th, passengers returning
n the stage which arriv-
They traveled exten-
gh the states, spending
in balmy California
the outside cities Mr,
or, "Dick" as he is
many Dawson friends
attle is the only city on
re there is any life and
sour dough can feel at
hing is running exter-
ible lat it is "on the
rooked or "short card"
tolerated. In all other
tie is far ahead of all
cities, the business be-
ice and the citizens be-
terms with themselves
at large.
hotel in San Francisco
cupied by Mr. and Mrs.
was entered by a thief
a window and a fire
McAndrews awoke but by
came aware of the pres-
and fellow was going
window, having been
way before he succeeded
his search of their
however, he managed to

ur Order!

ved with the
ne of samples
the Territory
h and French Mfg.

THE NEW KLONDIKE KING.

get away with a nugget bracelet
worth $100 and belonging to Mrs.
McAndrews, which was taken from a
pocket of her husband's clothes. In
his haste to get out the thief over-
looked a roll of bills and a well-filled
poke in "Dick's" pants pockets.
Tommy McDonald, another well-
known Dawsonite, also had in San
Francisco experience similar to that
of the man who fell among thieves on
his way to Jericho. Tommy was out-

PATRON ST. VALENTINE

Today the Favorite of
Youthful Lovers.

CITIZENS AROUS

Entire Country Indignant
Monstrous Treadgold C
cession Robbery.

MASS MEETING ON MONDAY

Protest to Be Wired to Con
ioner Ross.

BLIGHT ON THE TERRI

Every Effort Will Be Made t
the Outrageous Order-in
Council Revoked

Never before in the history
Klondike and Yukon territo
there such a wave of righteous
nation swept over the coun
that which is now stirring
souls of one might say every
woman and child anent the in
order in-council which gives to
C. Treadgold and his fellow
tionaires the right to all vaca
unoccupied land on three of th
est creeks in this the richest-s
earth. Two days ago when the
was first made public the full
cance of the gift was scarcely
prehensible, it being of such
tude and so far reaching. By
was still thought that the in
ual miner would still be able to
within the concession in open
tition with the concessionaires
selves, it having previously bee
that they, too, in order to
title to any claim must stal
apply for record the same as a
miner. According to the gold
mission's interpretation of th
der, however, the three creeks
together with all their tributar
closed entirely and everythin
which a grant was not issued
to January 1, 1902, clear from
mill to summit, is turned ov
Treadgold and his associates
may, if they so choose, not sp
dollar in the development of
monstrous gift for two years,
which time the public domain
has been presented to them lie
for they are prohibited from wo
any of their claims until certai
ditions have been previously ful
And what is required of them

By 1903, the Treadgold Concession spelled victory for the large consolidated mining company, and loss for the individual claim owner. (Klondike Nugget, 14 February 1902.)

July 4 1908

Sir

At 320 Front St next to the Dawson City Hotel there lives a woman who keeps a disorderly house (a prostitute) Formerly she had a Cigar License and was refused a new License this year and now she has located herself next door to the hotel and has a side door into the Alley where she solicits her patrons

She says the Sergeant is her friend and she need not go over the Bridge

Yours respectfully

Citizen

By 1908, prostitution had declined to the point that rumours that a woman was opening up shop could illicit a letter to the police. (Yukon Archives)

Dawson
23 3 1908

Sir

It may be of service to you to know that Banjo Nell - Miss Lewis, a well known Dance Hall frequenter and free lance has returned to Dawson for the purpose of reopening her Bluff Cigar Store

She has brought with her another woman and it is rumoured they propose opening two bluff stores on Front Street

Yours
Morality.

Major Wood
The Barracks
Dawson

M A P

OF THE

YUKON GOLDFIELDS.

SUPPLEMENT to the WEEKLY REPORT,
dated September 3, 1897.

E. SPIEGEL & CO., 120, Bishopsgate-str. Within, London, E.C.

Routes and Distances to Dawson City (Klondyke).

The White Pass Route.

	MILES
Victoria, B. C., or Seattle, U.S., to Taiya (Dyea) Inlet (Skagway Bay)	1,000
Taiya Inlet to White Pass	18
White Pass to White Horse Rapids	94
White Horse Rapids to Dawson City (Klondyke)	461
	1,563

The Taiya (Dyea) Pass Route.

	MILES
Victoria, B. C., or Seattle, U.S., to Taiya Inlet (Skagway Bay)	1,000
Taiya Inlet to Taiya Pass	15
Taiya Pass to White Horse Rapids	110
White Horse Rapids to Pelly River (Fort Selkirk)	278
Pelly River to Dawson City (Klondyke)	173
	1,578

The Yukon River Route.

	MILES
Victoria, B. C., or Seattle, U.S., to Dutch Harbour, Aleutian Islands	2,000
Dutch Harbour to St. Michael, Alaska	750
St. Michael to Dawson City (Klondyke)	1,650
	4,460

The Summit of Taiya Pass is 3,500 ft. above Sea Level.
The Summit of White Pass is about 2,500 ft. above Sea Level.

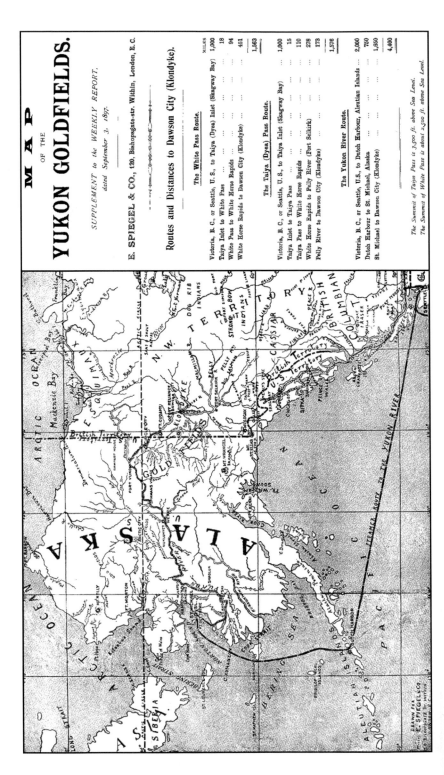

ABOVE – St. Andrew's Night, 1899. Not every activity at the Palace Grand
Theatre was as illicit as Diefenbaker's critics claimed. (Yukon Archives)

BELOW – Front Street, 1944. Dawson well after the rush, but before the federal government
started plans to convert the town into a "permanent living recreation" of the days of yore.

Diamond Tooth Gertie's—owned by Dawson City and operated by the Klondike Visitor's Association—is the only legalized gambling hall north of the sixtieth parallel. Can-can girls perform nightly and serve drinks as well. (Yukon Archives)

GENERAL MAP

Klondike Gold Fields, 1898, one of the richest gold strikes in the world. Gold was selling for approximately $15 to $16 an ounce. The exact amount of gold will never be known since there was a royalty to be evaded if possible, bu the Gold Commissioner estimated the output at $10 million in 1898 in 1898 increasing to $24 million in 1900 and then decling as Bonanza and Eldorado Creeks were mined out. (Yukon Archives)

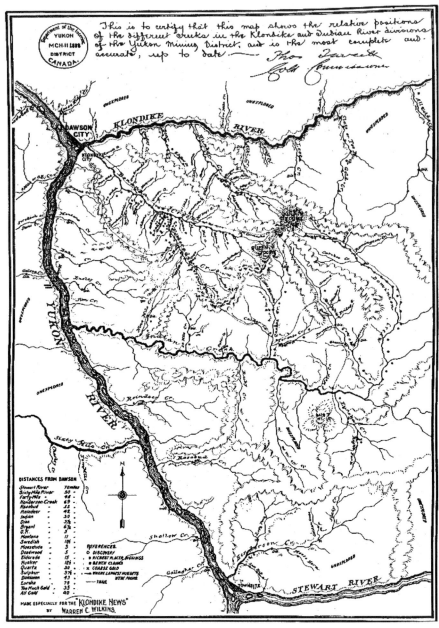

(Yukon Archives)

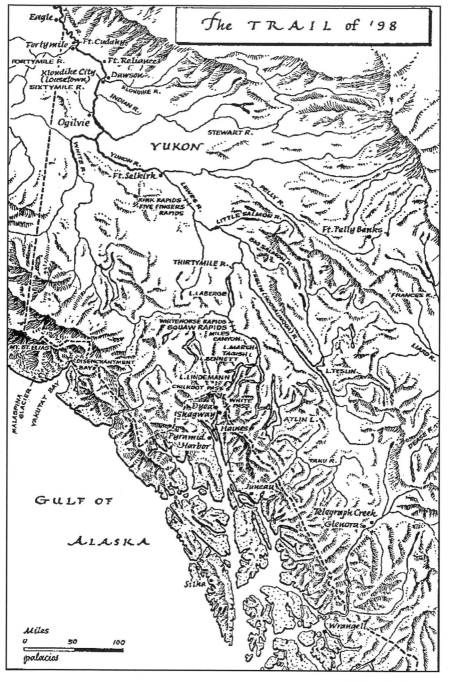

The TRAIL of '98

Eagle
Fortymile
FORTYMILE R.
Ft. Cudahy
Ft. Reliances
Klondike City
(Lousetown)
Dawson
SIXTYMILE R.
KLONDIKE R.
Ogilvie
INDIAN R.
STEWART R.
YUKON
WHITE R.
YUKON R.
Ft. Selkirk
RINK RAPIDS
FIVE FINGERS
RAPIDS
LEWES R.
PELLY R.
LITTLE SALMON R.
Ft. Pelly Banks
BIG SALMON R.
THIRTYMILE R.
FRANCES R.
L. LABERGE
TESLIN (HOOTALINQUA) R.
LIARD R.
WHITEHORSE RAPIDS
SQUAW RAPIDS
MILES
CANYON
L. MARCH
TAGISH L.
MT. ST. ELIAS
L. BENNETT
L. TESLIN
DISENCHANTMENT
BAY
L. LINDEMANN
CHILKOOT PASS
MALASPINA
GLACIER
YAKUTAT BAY
Dyea
Skagway
WHITE
PASS
Haines
ATLIN L.
DEASE R.
Pyramid
Harbor
TAKU R.
STIKINE R.
Juneau

GULF OF

ALASKA

Telegraph Creek
Glenora

Sitka

Wrangell

Miles
0   50   100
palacios

(Yukon Archives)

This map of Dawson—hand-drawn in 1903—depicts an orderly city with a strong commercial base. This was in stark contrast to the reality that Dawson was rapidly declining in the post-rush years.

committee of seven residents and property owners petitioned the mayor and police committee of the recently established city council. As chairman of the committee, Mr. Andrew Nerland expressed concern for the "demoralizing influence upon the little ones and one of repugnance and loathing on the part of the mothers." According to Nerland, "the women of whom the complaint is made have crowded among the homes without any respect to the decency of their surroundings by their carousals, vile language, and unseemly conduct." "Ladies and children are constantly exposed to sights not intended for their eyes," he declared.[4]

The other aspect of South-end concerns was that the influx of dissolute women to the vicinity would bring about a decline in property values and stunt commercial growth. Andrew Nerland was a partner of the signs and wallpaper firm of Anderson Brothers —a company that had recently spent thousands of dollars on property improvements. Nerland insisted that measures be taken to "preserve to the residents in that locality, the benefits of the business which by their energy and thrift has made it one of the most important business centres in Dawson."[5] The press agreed: "to hand over that portion of the city to a class that is lower than beasts is to compel respectable people to sacrifice their property that they have worked years to accumulate."[6]

Not every member of the police committee of the city council was empathetic with the residents of South Dawson. Alderman Murphy argued that the majority of people residing there had been in favour of the women moving to South Dawson in the first place, anticipating that they could sell or rent their property at a high figure. "Many had failed in the realization," Murphy contended—"hence the howl."[7] South Dawson was determined to be purified, though, and after the women were warned that their business was under the scrutiny of the NWMP, heavy policing and numerous arrests proved to be fairly effective in driving them out.

Economic and Political Developments

Property values were at the forefront of the grievances of South Dawson residents, but opposition to prostitution was also serving a more abstract purpose for them. It was at the time that Dawson's economy began to disintegrate that reform efforts took hold and the community attempted to attain an image of stability. As other historians have noted, inflated anxieties about social order and moral decay have surfaced in times of economic uncertainty—a hallmark of mining communities. Prostitutes become easy scapegoats for the complicated problems associated with economic decline.[8]

Despite rapid depopulation and the downturn in gold production in the Klondike after 1901, some optimism about Dawson's future had persisted. "This city, which seems so insignificant beside the great cities of Europe and America, contains within itself the germs of such an industrial and political expansion as the world never saw,"[9] predicted a grade seven student in her entry for an essay contest on the future of Dawson. In February 1902, a front-page political cartoon heralded a forecast of Dawson's future replete with a refined-looking woman surrounded by a vast expanse of trains, mining equipment, and industrial smokestacks.[10]

The day after this cartoon was printed, however, an economically devastating federal government decision was announced. Ottawa—under Minister of the Interior Clifford Sifton's direction—gave rights to all abandoned claims on Bonanza, Bear, and Hunker Creeks to a hydraulic mining syndicate headed by British mining expert A.N.C. Treadgold.[11] There is evidence that Sifton was part of the scheme. Treadgold allegedly wrote letters to Sifton indicating that he was buying creek claims in other names. Treadgold further requested that Sifton keep the royalty on gold high to drive out the remaining miners.[12]

As early as 1898 large consolidated mining companies had begun to dominate gold mining in the Yukon, but the

Treadgold concession was a further blow for Dawson. Prior to the announcement, Dawson and the Yukon Territory were inching towards increased political autonomy. Dawson was incorporated in December 1901 and had a wholly elected council by February 1902.[13] Political gains were also made at the territorial level. First, the federal government responded to demands for lower transportation costs by forcing the White Pass Yukon Route to decrease freight rates. Further, the House of Commons passed two acts in May 1902 concerning the territory. One gave the Yukon a representative to the House of Commons and added three elected members to the Yukon Council; the other lowered the royalty on placer gold.[14]

At this ironic juncture of political progress and economic uncertainty in the Yukon, the crusade against the "brazen women" of Dawson became a quest for control in unfamiliar territory.

The Scarlet Coat of the Law

In response to increasing public hostility toward prostitutes, the NWMP made many arrests. In some cases, members of the force over-extended the limits of their jurisdiction or loosened definitions of a criminal offence in order to get their woman. The case of Pauline Berge and Margaret Benoit is but one example. The two were apprehended by Constables Mallett and Wright and charged with streetwalking in Dawson. Their banishment to Klondike City was cutting into profits, so they began making visits into Dawson to solicit customers. NWMP inspector Wroughton gave Benoit and Berge six months of hard labour with no option of a fine, and told them that his sentence was intended to be a deterrent to others of their class.[15]

Two months later, however, Pauline Berge and Margaret Benoit won an appeal in the territorial court. Judge Craig maintained that in order for the officers to make an arrest and for the Crown to prosecute, the women would have to have been arrested at the time that they were *actually* accosting men. According to the Criminal Code, Judge Craig held, all three elements of the offence of streetwalking had to be proven: first, that the woman is a common prostitute, second, that she was wandering in the public street, and, third, that she did not give a satisfactory account of herself. "The demand must be made upon her for a satisfactory account before the arrest," he emphasized. Judge Craig argued, "It could not be contended for a moment that this unfortunate class of people are not allowed to walk the streets...for this would mean imprisonment in their homes." "This class of people", he concluded, "have the same rights on the streets as anybody else."[16]

The fact that NWMP inspector Wroughton acted as police magistrate may have contributed to the success of the appeal made by Benoit and Berge. Not only did members of the force arrest and prosecute women, but they occasionally tried them as well. This often did not work in favour of the accused. In 1904, Fred White, the comptroller of the RNWMP in Ottawa, was told that there was "exception taken" to the practice of officers holding court—especially since there were three judges living in Dawson. Over a third of the court sessions were held by RNWMP officers. "Personally I think it is a good thing to allow the Police to act occasionally, as it gives our officers a lot of experience, but apparently it has been a little overdone in Dawson and Whitehorse," White admitted.[17] Inspector Wroughton, for example, had held court for two months in 1902 when police magistrate Macaulay was away. It is significant that Wroughton was acting police magistrate when over twenty women were charged within the short span of a week for streetwalking and setting up cigar stores in South Dawson.

Not all prostitutes were charged under the Criminal Code. At least a dozen South Dawson women were charged under the provisions of a city bylaw for the "preservation of peace and public morals" in the campaign of 1902. It was easier to prosecute women under a bylaw than to have to prove all the elements of a criminal offence—especially if arrests were made according to the more onerous standards of Judge Craig in the Benoit and Berge case. According to the Mounted Police Act of 1894, however, the NWMP were not supposed to enforce municipal bylaws at all. When it was discovered in 1903 that the police were doing so in the Yukon, changes were made to the Mounted Police Act.[18] The section that prohibited the NWMP from enforcing bylaws, the amendment stated, "shall not apply, and shall not be deemed to have heretofore applied, to the NWMP Force within the Yukon Territory."

Sexually suspect women were not the only targets of police over-zealousness during the campaign to clean up Dawson. A number of different racial and ethnic groups also failed to meet the reigning standards of respectability. They too had their day in court.

Regulating Race

For many local First Nations people, the gold rush was a purely destructive force. While stampeders to the Klondike struck it rich, the Hän suffered from disease, as well as from the effects of game and timber depletion. Policies were put in place to exclude Hän men from employment in placer mining.[19] After being uprooted from their traditional fishing grounds in Klondike City, many Hän moved one mile down the Yukon River to the mouth of Moosehide Creek. The Anglican Church purchased some land there and established the Moosehide Mission in 1897. "To abandon them now that the place is overrun by miners would involve their destruction by more than a relapse to heathenism, namely in their being swallowed up in the miner's temptations to drink, gambling and immorality," Bishop Bompas believed.[20]

Liquor infractions were probably the most common

reason that First Nations people were hauled into police court. It was an offence under the Indian Act of 1867 for an Aboriginal person to be intoxicated, as well as for a non-Aboriginal person to supply Aboriginal person with liquor.[21] "Firewater brings trouble to Native sons and daughters," it was proclaimed. The reference was to the "denizens of the forest" from "fish-scented moosehide" who had crowded into Magistrate Macaulay's courtroom to hear the cases of "Indian Annie" and "Indian Angus." Annie was sentenced to a fine of $10 or ten days of hard labour for being drunk. Angus was sentenced to forty-four days of hard labour for assaulting Annie and for drunkenness. It was agreed that he could be released if he disclosed who supplied him with the liquor.

When another group of Moosehide Indians appeared in police court, "Fat John, a thin cadaverous looking one who looks as though he is bilious and has night sweats and ringing in the ears," was charged with having provided one Louisa with whisky. The *Nugget* described the scene: "Chief Silas, son Billian, a stout, skookum buck of perhaps 18 winters, was asked to point out who furnished him with the liquor. 'Sitting there with the fur overcoat on,' said Billie, at the same time pointing a finger that knows not Pear's soap at John L. Labbe, proprietor of the Labbe Hotel and saloon on Queen St."[22] Dawsonites ridiculed the very people whose land they occupied, yet it was the stampeders who introduced alcohol to the Hän on a large scale.

Charges of "drunk and disorderly" were regular occurrences in the police court. They were applied to people from the gamut of racial and ethnic groups. What is clear, though, is that when the accused did not have white skin, racial commentary became the theme of the police court column. When two Japanese men "from the land of the Mikado" were found drunk in a snowbank, it was suggested that "too much Dawson hootch disturbs Oriental equilibriums." The men who "knew sufficient English to plead guilty" and were renamed Cado Juno Tabasco Sauso and Ketchup Yam Tomato Howso were given the option of a fine or twenty days of hard labour. Since they were unable to pay the fine, it was noted that "unless their countrymen come to their rescue there will be another case of Oriental labour."[23]

The anti-Asian sentiment of late-nineteenth-century North America tended to root itself in fears of Asian men flooding the labour market. In 1898, Dawson residents were assured that they need not worry as "no one as yet has noticed a Chinaman in town." The explanation was that "the climate would be decidedly unhealthy for any enterprising sons of the...Empire who might happen to stroll this way." It was presumed that "information to this effect has been sent down to the coast or Chinamen and pig tails and washe washe houses would long ago have been common sights in the streets of Dawson."[24]

But Chinese men were noticeable later that year. "Yes, we have 5 o'clock teas in Dawson City," Mrs. P. Sampson assured the readers of the *New York Times*. Attempting to describe a "civilised" division of labour, she added that "three steam laundries and three Chinamen now compete for this trade, with some wives of the poorer miners."[25] Asian men did not necessarily flock to the laundry or restaurant business out of personal choice, though. In Dawson, as in some other mining communities, labour policies were invoked to keep Chinese men out of the mines.[26] Occupations were therefore limited.

By 1902 there was a lobby to keep Asian labourers out of the Yukon altogether. In June of that year, five Chinese men travelling from Victoria, B.C. arrived in Whitehorse on the train from Skagway, Alaska. The men were seeking employment in the Yukon as cooks or launderers. The next morning, however, they were met by an inhospitable local committee who informed them that they were not welcome in the Yukon Territory. When the Chinese men expressed their desire to go to Dawson, the committee ordered them to leave on the freight train for Skagway in an hour's time. The committee proceeded to collect $200 from other Whitehorse residents to guarantee the men's passage to Victoria.[27]

"Respectable labourers" were scolded for frequenting

Chinese restaurants in Dawson. "How can the Labour Union ask the support of the merchants of Dawson to keep out the Chinese if labouring men continue to patronize these creatures?" the editor of the *Klondike Miner and Arctic Circle Herald* asked.[28]

The reform effort of 1902 was an attempt to draw the moral boundaries of post-rush Dawson. First Nations people, Chinese men, and "disreputable" women alike were expected to stay beyond the limits of an orderly town. The excitement of the gold rush had dissipated, though the remnants of vice were still politically charged in the years ahead.

Chapter 7

The Calming of the Klondike

The "moral flood" of 1902 helped to purge the Territory of disreputables, but depopulation also played a significant role. The population declined steadily after the rush. Weary travellers returned home empty-handed, though a lucky few had gold lining their pockets. Gold-seekers with more stamina joined the exodus to other gold strikes in regions less adulterated by the presence of large mining corporations—Nome, Alaska in 1899 and the Tanana River (Fairbanks) in 1903. What was once the largest city west of Winnipeg was already a shadow of its former glory.

Certainly there was "less sin because there were far fewer sinners"[1] in the Klondike, but Dawson had also made a transformation from a mining camp to an established town in the post-rush years. By 1903, Dawson was still a miners' town, but the increasing ratio of families to single men, the more prominent presence of the RNWMP, and an elected municipal government were signs of a more matured community—at least in the social and political, since not in the economic, sense. As though responding to Kate Heaman's letter of 1900 on behalf of the WCTU, a Dawson social columnist declared in 1903:

> good order prevails on the creek. The boys who are nearly all bachelors are sober, industrious and well behaved members of society. Whether this excellent characteristic is to be attributed to their own innate manliness, to the splendid police

supervision maintained, or to the presence of so many estimable ladies, or to a combination of all three facts...your correspondent is unable to determine.[2]

Dawson—once described as "gold, whisky, and women in a riotous whirl"[3]—had been sedated by depopulation and moral reform.

Prostitution still lingered, of course, though on a smaller scale. The RNWMP and the chief license inspector were able to keep prostitution and other vestiges of vice at bay with a new device—the Liquor License Ordinance. Prostitution—a subject that was formerly discussed in the papers on a regular basis, and petitioned against by "respectable citizens"—was now, for the most part, relegated to correspondence between the police, the liquor license inspector, and the Yukon commissioner.

"In the Interests of Sobriety and Morality"

Recognizing that the dance-halls (licensed until 1902 and between 1904 and 1907) were a hotbed of prostitution, the arm of the law was able to reach the social evil with the Liquor License Ordinance. Instead of targeting the women directly, the Ordinance smoked them out. Licensed establishments had their license cancelled—or were at least threatened to have them cancelled—if they infringed the parts of the Ordinance that related to prostitution.

The Liquor License Ordinance was passed in 1899 by the Yukon Council. Its purpose was to regulate liquor sales and to generate revenue for the territorial and federal governments through licensing fees. From the outset, though, the Ordinance had an ulterior motive: to control prostitution. In 1899, some businessmen regarded the practice of prostitutes selling liquor in their cabins as a threat to "legitimate" liquor sales. These men urged the territorial government to pass the Ordinance, believing that the high cost of obtaining a license would drive the women out of business.

Subsequent amendments to the Liquor License Ordinance in 1902 were more overt in their intention to curb prostitution. Two sections were added that were designed to end the practice of dance-hall women earning a percentage on liquor sales for dancing with men. For one, there could be no public dancing on licensed premises, and secondly, there could be no connection between a dance-hall and licensed premises. A third section stated that no woman "suspected of being a prostitute" was allowed in licensed premises.

In 1904, chief license inspector Arthur Wilson pointed out the roadblock to making a conviction under the ordinance against licensed premises that paid women a percentage: "it is almost impossible to obtain truthful statements from these kind of women...and as we have to depend entirely to secure a conviction upon the evidence obtained from the women themselves or from the licensee...a conviction is very difficult." However, it was in fact quite simple for the chief license inspector or the RNWMP to cancel or refuse to renew a license. They had only to find a woman *suspected* of being a prostitute on the premises. The definition of such a woman was at their discretion.[4]

These prosecutions did not always hold up in court. One judge held that the bartender or proprietor had to *know* that the woman was a dance-hall woman.[5] Nonetheless, several licenses were cancelled for this reason. The RNWMP admitted that it was much easier to discourage prostitution through the dance-halls and saloons than it was to convict women under the Criminal Code.

The crackdown on prostitution in 1902 was facilitated by the bylaw for "the preservation of peace and public morals." It took less evidence and effort to prosecute a woman for infringing a bylaw than for violating the Criminal Code. It was later discovered that the RNWMP did not even have the jurisdiction to enforce bylaws. The Mounted

Police Act had to be retroactively amended to rectify this. Similarly, in 1908 it was pointed out that it might not be appropriate for the Force to have the burden of enforcing the Liquor License Ordinance. "In the early days the R.N.W.M. Police enforced law and order just as they do in Dawson today, yet had nothing to do with breaches of the Liquor License Ordinance, which were dealt with by the Liquor Inspector alone," complained Major Wood.[6] Considering that the Ordinance served as a quasi Criminal Code, however, it did seem fitting that in these later years it was enforced by the police.

In August 1904, the Liquor License Ordinance was altered once again. Women deemed to be prostitutes were still excluded from licensed premises—at least officially—but the sections of the Ordinance that effectively de-licensed the dance-halls were repealed. It appeared that the Ordinance had been relaxed, but in truth, the authorities were unwilling to relinquish their handle on iniquity. When the dance-halls were not licensed, there was no official control over the proprietors or their employees.[7] The Ordinance was a valuable tool with which to stamp out vice.

With the Ordinance in effect, rampant vice in the Klondike seemed to be a problem of the past. That is, until 1907 when Reverend John Pringle, a Presbyterian minister and former member of the Yukon Council appeared on the scene. Dawson is "an open and offensive moral sewer," he alerted the Prime Minister, as well as the Montreal, Toronto, Ottawa, and Vancouver newspapers. Thanks to Pringle, the issue of vice in the Klondike flared up again on a national scale. An investigation was launched by the Department of Justice, and the 1907 equivalent of Question Period was loaded with accusations about the Liberal government's administration of the Yukon Territory.

Men like Arthur Wilson who had gone to great lengths to clean up the dance-halls were furious. Pringle, Wilson cried, had printed "some of the most ridiculous statements that are as far from the real fact as is possible for a prejudicial mind to conceive or a fictions pen to describe."[8] "Knowing the Pacific Coast from Southern California, to the North," the owners of the M&N and Flora Dora dance-halls insisted, "there cannot be found one music hall conducted in so orderly a manner and containing the same class of women as are to be found in these two halls in Dawson."[9]

Reverend Pringle's post-gold-rush crusade against immorality was directed at dance-halls as well as at certain Yukon officials. These men not only allowed vice to persist, he believed, but were perpetrators of sin themselves. Pringle wrote to Prime Minister Wilfrid Laurier in July 1907:

> I would again, and for the last time, call your attention to the drunkenness and lust in official circles here, which are the open scandal of the city and Territory.... [Mr. Girouard] lives in open fornication with his female partner...and Mr. Lithgow companies with harlots in the dance-halls, is drunk and openly and frequently in our streets and when in his condition exposes his person in broad daylight before the eyes of decent men and women...dance-halls and bawdy houses are the natural concomitants of the presence in our administrative life of unashamed male prostitutes.[10]

Pringle warned the Prime Minister: "I have resolved, if this continues as at present, to state the case in the plainest terms in the Eastern press, without regard to the notoriety and discomfort which such disclosures may bring to myself."[11]

Most prominent Yukoners believed that Pringle's diatribes were politically, rather than spiritually, motivated. The *Dawson News* declared that his actions were "a vulgar attempt to vent political spleen." This was entirely accurate. Pringle, it was speculated, turned against the federal Liberal government when he was not appointed commissioner of the Yukon.[12] He was also embittered when he failed to secure the federal Liberal nomination for the Yukon in

1904.[13] It is not completely clear why J.T. Lithgow (comptroller of the Yukon from 1898 to 1911 and Yukon councillor from 1904 to 1908) and J.E. Girouard (Registrar of Lands and Yukon councillor, 1898-1908) became the targets of his reprisal. However, both men were candidates for the commissionership in 1907 and Pringle and Girouard (who later sued for libel) were fellow Yukon councillors from 1903 to 1904. During his term, Pringle had a conflict with the council when he was not awarded his sessional indemnity due to his prolonged absence from the Territory.[14]

It is also plausible that Pringle's aspirations lay in a promotion within the church and a desire to move from the dwindling community of Grand Forks. After his newspaper campaign and tour in the East, Pringle left the Klondike permanently in March 1908 and went on to a new church with a larger parish in Sydney, Nova Scotia.[15] At the General Meeting of the Presbyterian Church of Canada in that year, Pringle received his reward: he was honoured with a resolution that praised his "fearless denunciation of vice."[16]

In addition to providing fodder for the federal Conservative Opposition in Parliament, Pringle's allegations elicited a local defence of the Yukon's moral reputation. The Anglican Bishop in Dawson had "no desire to enter newspaper controversies" but was compelled to maintain that "these false insinuations and allegations can't go on forever without some contradictions."[17] Pringle was rebuked by the Board of Trade, and the entire Yukon Council (with the exception of Conservative George Black) united to pass a resolution officially condemning Pringle. Dr. La Chapelle reiterated the Yukon Council's belief that "Dawson will compare favourably with any part of America and with any town in the respect paid to law and order, the regard for morality and the observance of all social, commercial, legal and religious conventions, decencies and amenities."[18] During the debate, Councillor John Grant exclaimed: "Mr. Pringle is a puritanical hypocrite and a coat of tar and feathers would fit him better than the praise which has been accorded him on the outside."[19] Grant (member for South Dawson) proceeded to introduce an affidavit, signed by a prostitute, that alleged that the Reverend himself had consorted with lewd women.[20] In his year-end report, Major Wood referred to Pringle's accusations and emphasized that they were based on "occurrences several years old" when the Klondike was "outside the bounds of refined civilisation."[21]

John Pringle's colleagues of the council and of the cloth emphasized that he had never complained through local channels about "vice" in the Klondike—either in his capacity as Yukon councillor or as a Presbyterian minister in Grand Forks. "Dr. Pringle sat for two years as a member of the Yukon Council and we do not recollect that at that time, when there was a possibility of another nomination, that he ever lifted his voice very loudly against these places of amusement which since he has resumed his clerical garb and habit he finds to be so iniquitous," two dance-hall owners noted.[22]

Pringle took his crusade to the traditional guardians of morality in the North—the East. Accordingly, his critics made comparisons. "The town has been as free from immorality as an Eastern City, and much more so than in any other mining camp that has hitherto been known," quipped Major Wood.[23] In past years, Yukon officials had deflected the grievances of the WCTU and Clifford Sifton's Department of the Interior. Since then, Dawson residents had demonstrated that they were quite capable of suppressing vice on their own. They were proud of their efforts and resented outside interference.

As though echoing his predecessor, Minister of the Interior Frank Oliver told the Yukon commissioner that in light of the investigation sparked by Reverend Pringle's remarks, he was ordered to amend the Liquor License Ordinance so as to "prevent the serving of liquor in any place of public entertainment...and to secure the prohibition of the serving of liquor or the attendance in the ordering of liquor by women."[24]

Moral reputations, difficult as they were to establish, were equally hard to maintain.

CONCLUSION

The questionable reputation of the Yukon was not to resurface again for another half century. In 1959, the Conservative government under John Diefenbaker announced its plan to revive the struggling community of Dawson. The town was in need of a boost. The capital of the Yukon had been changed from Dawson to Whitehorse in 1953, partly because the Alaska Highway built during World War II bypassed Dawson altogether. Further, increased operation costs and fixed gold prices signalled the end of any remnants of large scale gold mining in the Klondike region. During an April 1959 visit to Dawson, however, Diefenbaker discovered a new resource—tourism. The prime minister recognized the tourist appeal of the Palace Grand Theatre, and before long, plans were under way to unveil the reconstructed dance-hall at the Dawson City Festival set for July 1962.

The idea of economic development was certainly respectable, but it was the means that were criticized by the Liberal opposition. A place once renowned for liquor, gambling, and "painted dancers" would make for a decidedly lewd national historic site, the Liberals argued. Immorality in the Klondike gold rush became the subject of lively House of Commons debates a remarkable sixty years after the event, and Diefenbaker's government was put on the defensive. Conservative M.P. Walter Dinsdale assured dubious opposition member Jack Pickersgill that the decision to declare the Palace Grand Theatre a national historic site "was made by a no less distinguished group than the Historic Sites and Monuments Board, which includes some of the most distinguished historians in Canada."[1] Dinsdale reminded the House that some of the "indecent" activities that had gone on in the theatre at the time of the rush had occurred when the Yukon had been under a "Liberal Regime." The honourable member promised the Opposition that "every activity that takes place...will be highly respectable."[2]

The Dawson City Festival—staged by Tom Patterson, the mastermind of the Stratford Festival— was only the beginning. Today the entire town has taken on a gold rush theme, and nearly every establishment boasts a brightly painted false front. Dawson City is meant to be a living recreation of the gold rush. Interestingly, the gold rush of a hundred years past is still able to prompt community debates. These include whether the can-can girls are appropriate "ambassadors" of the Yukon, whether the gold panner is a relevant symbol on modern licence plates, and whether a main street in Whitehorse should be named "Jack London Boulevard." Kwanlin Dun First Nation, among others, successfully resisted the change, not only because of London's social Darwinist views on race, but because the gold rush focus of Yukon culture has been a little overdone.[3]

The can-can girl, however, still retains her powerful tenure. Since 1970, she has been performing her nightly routine during the tourist season at Diamond Tooth Gertie's gambling casino—the only legalized casino north of the 60th parallel. Surely the civic boosters of the post-rush period would be horrified to witness the Dawson of the present actually *celebrating* the vices of gamblers and painted ladies in their plan of economic development. Under the guise of history, the rowdy atmosphere of the past is now benign family fun as a tourist attraction. Meanwhile, the can-can girl—the official symbol of Dawson City—kicks up the dirt from the past of what once was a booming, northern frontier mining town.

Endnotes

Introduction

1. *Dawson City Map: Attractions and Service Guide*, 1993.
2. *Yukon News*, 18 March 1992.
3. William Morrison, "Policing the Boomtown: The Mounted Police as a Social Force in the Klondike," *Northern Review* (Winter 1990), p. 84.
4. Barbara Kelcey, "Lost in the Rush: The Forgotten Women of the Klondike Gold Rush" (M.A. thesis: University of Victoria, 1987), p. 202. For more on women in the Klondike, see Melanie Mayer, *Klondike Women: True Tales of the 1897–1898 Gold Rush* (Ohio: Swallow Press/Ohio University Press, 1989).
5. Robert Service, *The Trail of '98: A Northland Romance* (Toronto: William Briggs, 1911), pp. 369–70.

Chapter 1

1. Ken S. Coates and William R. Morrison, *Land of the Midnight Sun: A History of the Yukon* (Edmonton: Hurtig Publishers, 1988), p. 85. Initially, these people would have taken a steamer from Dawson to St. Michael, Alaska, at which point they could connect with steamers heading south.
2. William Morrison, *Showing the Flag: The Mounted Police and Canadian Sovereignty in the North, 1894–1925* (Vancouver: University of British Columbia Press, 1985), p. 32.
3. For more on the Chilkoot Trail and Yukon First Nations, see David Neufeld and Frank Norris, *Chilkoot Trail: Heritage Route to the Klondike* (Whitehorse: Lost Moose Publishers, 1997).
4. Coates and Morrison, *Land of the Midnight Sun*, p. 112; Catherine McClellan, *Part of the Land, Part of the Water: A History of the Yukon Indians* (Vancouver: Douglas & McIntyre, 1987), pp. 169–70; "Forgotten Claims," *Canadian Geographic*, November/December 1996, pp. 36–48.

5. Ken Coates, *Best Left as Indians: Native-White Relations in the Yukon Territory, 1840–1973* (Montreal: McGill-Queen's Press, 1991), pp. 42–45, 110.
6. Coates and Morrison, *Land of the Midnight Sun*, p. 146.

Chapter 2

1. Laura Berton, *I Married the Klondike* (Toronto: Little, Brown, 1954), p. 82.
2. Carolyn Strange, "From 'Modern Babylon' to the 'City on the Hill'" in *Patterns of the Past: Interpreting Ontario's History* (Toronto: Dundurn Press, 1988), p. 261; Mariana Valverde, *The Age of Light, Soap and Water: Moral Reform in English Canada, 1885–1925* (Toronto: McClelland & Stewart, 1991); Wendy Mitchinson, "'For God, Home and Native Land': A Study in Nineteenth-Century Feminism" in *A Not Unreasonable Claim: Women and Reform in Canada, 1880's–1920's*, ed. Linda Kealey (Toronto: Women's Educational Press, 1979).
3. WCTU Archives, World WCTU Report of the 6th Convention, 1898, Toronto, quoted in John McLaren, "'White Slavers': The Reform of Canada's Prostitution Laws and Patterns of Enforcement, 1900–1920," paper presented at the meeting of the American Society for Legal History, Faculty of Law, University of Toronto, 23–25 October, 1986, p. 33.
4. This was especially true in the "white slave panic." By 1910, "white slavery" came to dominate debates about prostitution in Canada, the United States, and Western Europe. During this period of moral panic, it was believed that almost any female was susceptible to being lured into the international traffic in women—especially by a "foreign" procurer. See Valverde, *Age of Light, Soap and Water*, p. 103; Ruth Rosen, *The Lost Sisterhood: Prostitution in America, 1900–1918* (Baltimore: Johns Hopkins University Press, 1982), p. 3.
5. Strange, "From 'Modern Babylon'," p. 255.
6. Mary Lee Davis, *Sourdough Gold: The Log of a Yukon Adventure* (Boston, 1933), p. 103.
7. NAC, RCMP RG 18, D4, v. l, Police Gaol Record 1900–1902.
8. *KN*, 14 July 1900.
9. *KN*, 26 February 1902.
10. *KN*, 2 April 1902; NAC, RCMP RG 18, D4, v. l, Police Gaol Record 1900–1902.
11. NAC, RCMP RG 18, D4, v. l, Police Gaol Record 1900–1902.
12. YA, GR Series 11, Vol. 1435, f. 8; NAC, RCMP RG 18, D4, v. l, Police Gaol Record 1900–1902; *KN*, 10 November 1902.
13. *KN*, 11 July 1902.

14. *KN*, 26 November 1898.

15. *KN*, 15–17 April 1902; *Dawson Daily News*, 18 April 1902.

16. RNWMP Inspector Wroughton to Acting Commissioner, 14 February 1908, YA, YGR Series 1, v. 9, f. 1443.

17. YA, GOV 1431, f. 7.

18. NAC, RCMP RG 18, D4, v.l, Police Gaol Record 1900–1902.

19. *KN*, 18 September 1902.

20. *KN*, 17 April 1902.

21. *KN*, 25 March 1902.

22. *KN*, 18 April 1903.

23. YA, YGR Series 11, v. 1433, f. 6.

24. Inspector Wroughton to Assistant Commissioner, 7 December 1907, YA, YGR Series 1, v. 9, f. 1443, GOV 1619.

25. Davis, *Sourdough Gold*, p. 184.

26. *KN*, 14 May 1903.

27. YA, YGR Series 11, v. 1433, f. 6.

28. A.N.C. Treadgold, *Report on the Goldfields of the Klondike* (Toronto: George N. Morang, 1899).

29. YA, GOV 1431, f. 7.

30. License Inspector to Chief License Inspector, 2 May 1904, YA, YGR Series 1, v. 9, f. 1443.

31. YA, YGR 15, v. 4, f. 383.

32. "Klondike Kate Given Shock by Girls of 1937—Famous Character of Gold Rush Days Views Generation With Alarm," *Daily Alaska Empire*, 13 December 1937 (wired from the *Seattle Post-Intelligencer*). Kate spent her summers in Dawson with her husband, Johnny Matson, who operated a small mine there.

33. Sgt. McMillan to Officer Commanding, NWMP, 7 December 1907, YA, YGR Series 1, v. 9, f. 1443.

34. Wood to Ogilvie, 18 July 1900, YA, YGR Series 1, V. 9, F. 1443.

35. Ordinance of 1902, "An Ordinance Respecting Intoxicating Liquors."

36. YA, GOV 1431, f. 7.

37. Ibid.

38. Sgt. McMillan to Officer Commanding, 7 December 1907. YA, YGR Series 1, v. 9, f. 1443, GOV 1619.

39. *KN*, May 1903.

40. On May 3, 1899 it was reported in the *Nugget* that a man had found a fetus wrapped in newspaper, in a pasteboard box, hidden under a rock. Given that contraception was virtually non-existent, women would have been occasionally forced to resort to self-induced abortions.

    In her study of prostitution on the Comstock Lode, Marion Goldman documents the use of contraceptive douches and abortifacients, many of which were lethal. Infanticide was also fairly frequent in late-nineteenth-century Nevada. Marion Goldman, *Gold Diggers and Silver Miners: Prostitution and Social Life on the Comstock Lode* (Ann Arbour: University of Michigan Press, 1981), pp. 125–29.

41. *KN*, 21 December 1898. The "strychnine route" is a word play on the Stikine River route—a less-travelled water and land route to the Klondike via the Alaskan panhandle and northern B.C.

42. *KN*, 14 December 1898.

43. See also, Susan Johnston, "Twice Slain: Female Sex Trade Workers and Suicide in British Columbia, 1870–1920," paper presented to the annual conference of the Canadian Historical Association, Calgary, June 1994; Goldman, *Gold Diggers and Silver Miners*, p. 128.

44. *KN*, 19 April 1902.

45. *KN*, 2 May 1902. Some studies of mining communities in the American West indicate that there was segregation of Black or Chinese prostitutes, though there is no evidence of this in the Klondike. See Goldman, *Gold Diggers and Silver Miners*; Paula Petrak, *No Step Backwards: Women and Family on the Rocky Mountain Mining Frontier, Helena, Montana, 1865–1900* (Helena: Montana Historical Press Society, 1987); Anne M. Butler, *Daughters of Joy, Sisters of Mercy: Prostitutes in the American West, 1865–1890* (Chicago: University of Illinois Press, 1985).

44. Ken S. Coates and William R. Morrison, *Land of the Midnight Sun: A History of the Yukon* (Edmonton: Hurtig Publishers, 1988), p. 110.

45. Josiah Spurr, *Through the Yukon Gold Diggings* (Boston, 1900) quoted in Michael Gates, *Gold at Fortvmile Creek: Early Days in the Yukon* (Vancouver: University of British Columbia Press, 1994), p. 80.

Chapter 3

1. *KN*, 5 November 1898.

2. James H. Gray, *Red Lights on the Prairies* (Toronto: Macmillan of Canada, 1971), p. 11.

3. Ruth Rosen, *The Lost Sisterhood: Prostitution in America, 1900–1918* (Baltimore: Johns Hopkins University Press, 1982), p. 21.

4. John d'Emilio and Estelle Freedman, *Intimate Matters: A History of Sexuality in America* (New York: Harper and Row, 1988), p.132.; Timothy Gilfoyle, *City of Eros: New York City, Prostitution and the Commercialization of Sex, 1790–1920* (New York and London: W.W. Norton and Company, 1992), p. 265.

5. For more on men and morality in resource-based communities,

see Karen Dubinsky, *Improper Advances: Rape and Heterosexual Conflict in Ontario, 1880–1929* (Chicago: University of Chicago Press, 1993); Nancy Forestell, "'All That Glitters is Not Gold': The Gendered Dimensions of Work, Family, and Community Life in the Northern Ontario Gold Mining Town of Timmins, 1909–1950" (Ph.D. dissertation, University of Toronto, 1993).

6. *The War Cry*, 26 March 1898.

7. Susan Lee Johnson, "Bulls, Bears, and Dancing Boys: Race, Gender, and Leisure in the California Gold Rush," *Radical History Review* 60 (1994): 19. For more on male homosocial working-class culture, see Forestell, "All That Glitters"; for male saloon culture on the Rocky Mountain mining frontier, see Elliott West, *The Saloon on the Rocky Mountain Mining Frontier* (Lincoln: University of Nebraska Press, 1979).

8. Proprietors to Minister of Justice, April 1907. YA, YGR Series 1, v. 9, f. 1443.

9. *KN*, 28 February 1901.

10. YA, GOV 1431, f. 7, *R. v. May Fields*.

11. Sex between men had the potential to stir controversy and solicit police intervention. In July 1904, Patrick Penny and Richard Ashcroft Jones shared a bed in Penny's cabin for the night (this would not have been uncommon with housing and shelter shortages). The next day Jones made a complaint to the police and Penny was charged with "intent to commit sodomy." Interestingly, each man testified that it was the other who had made the sexual advances in bed and Penny maintained that Jones had sought charges because he had failed to "get his own way." YA, GOV 1440, f. 7. See also, D'Emilio and Freedman, *Intimate Matters*, p. 124; Gary Kinsman, *The Regulation of Desire: Sexuality in Canada* (Montreal: Black Rose Books, 1987), p. 77.

12. *KN*, 18 April 1903.

13. *KN*, 4 October 1899.

14. YA, GR Series 11, v. 1435, f. 8.

15. Detective Welsh to Officer Commanding, 25 August 1905. YA, YGR Series 1, v. 9, f. 1443.

16. Sgt. McMillan to Officer Commanding, 7 December 1907. YA, YGR Series 1, v. 9, f. 1443.

17. Proprietors to Minister of Justice, 8 April 1907. YA, YGR Series 1, v. 9, f. 1443.

18. *KN*, 7 March 1901.

19. *KN*, 8 July 1899.

20. *KN*, 20 June 1902.

21. Ibid.

22. YA, GR Series 11, v. 1472, f. 50.

23. *KN*, 6 Decmeber 1902.

Chapter 4

1. *Klondike Nugget*, 4 November 1899.
2. *KN*, 12 June 1899.
3. *KN*, 12 June 1899.
4. *KN*, 4 November 1899.
5. *KN*, 3 March, 1901.
6. NAC, RCMP RG 18, D4, v. 1, Police Gaol Record 1902.
7. Ibid.
8. *KN*, 21 January 1899.
9. *KN*, 20 May 1903.
10. *KN*, 2 July 1903.
11. *KN*, 11 May 1903.
12. *KN*, 12 May 1903.
13. John McLaren, "Chasing the Social Evil: Moral Fervour and the Evolution of Canada's Prostitution Laws, 1867–1917," *Canadian Journal of Law and Society*, 1 (1986): 139.
14. Emma Goldman, *Living My Life*, vol. 1 (New York: Dover, 1970), quoted in Ruth Rosen, *The Lost Sisterhood: Prostitution in America, 1900–1918* (Baltimore: Johns Hopkins University Press, 1982) p. 109.
15. F.C. Wade to E.L. Newcombe, Toronto, 13 November 1901. NAC, RG 18, v. 219, f. 905.
16. F.C. Wade, response to NWMP Comptroller Fred White, 26 February 1901. NAC, RG 18, v. 219, f. 905.
17. Hal Guest, "A History of Dawson City," Microfiche Report Series 181 (Ottawa: Parks Canada, 1985), p. 225.
18. Timothy Gilfoyle, *City of Eros: New York City, Prostitution and the Commercialisation of Sex, 1790–1920* (New York and London: W.W. Norton and Company, 1992), p. 265.
19. NAC, YTR RG 91, v. 23, f. 6551.
20. YA, GOV 1431, f. 7, *R*. v. *Fields*.
21. Smart to Ogilvie, 22 November 1900, YA, YGR Series 1, v. 9, f. 1443.
22. Ogilvie to Smart, 27 December 1900, YA, YGR Series 1, v. 9, f. 1443.
23. D.J. Hall, *Clifford Sifton: The Young Napoleon* (Vancouver: University of British Columbia Press, 1981), pp. 191, 295.
24. YA, YGR Series 1, v. 9, f. 1443, GOV 1619, 10 July 1902.
25. Wade may have associated George DeLeon with Daniel DeLeon, a prominent American socialist of the era. Paul Buhle, *Marxism in the United States* (London: Verso, 1987), p. 50.
26. *KN*, 7 January 1902.
27. David Morrison, *The Politics of the Yukon Territory: 1898–1909* (Toronto: University of Toronto Press, 1968), p. 23; Hall, *Clifford Sifton*, p. 191.

Chapter 5

1. *San Francisco Examiner*, 6 October 1897, quoted in Hal Guest, "A History of Dawson City," Microfiche Report Series 181 (Ottawa: Parks Canada, 1985), p. 16.
2. As quoted in Hal Guest, "Dawson City, San Francisco of the North or Boomtown in a Bog: A Literature Review," Manuscript Report Series 241 (Ottawa: Parks Canada, 1978), p. 13.
3. Rex Beach, *The Spoilers* (Toronto: Poole, 1906), quoted in William Keith Hubbard, "The Klondike Gold Rush in Literature, 1896–1930," M.A. thesis, University of Western Ontario, 1969, p. 104.
4. Mary Lee Davis, *Sourdough Gold: The Log of a Yukon Adventure* (Boston, 1933), p. 183.
5. *KN*, 14 September 1898.
6. *KN*, 16 April 1902.
7. Guest, "A History," p. 221.
8. NAC, RCMP Records, v. 3055; *KN*, 12 October 1898, cited in Guest, "A History," p. 221.
9. A.B. Perry to Sifton, 7 November 1899, University of Manitoba Library, Sifton Papers, reel c493, cited in Guest, "A History," p. 221.
10. *KN*, 26 November 1898.
11. Sulfa drugs were not used as a cure for gonorrhea and syphilis until the 1930s. Allan Brandt, *No Magic Bullet: A Social History of Venereal Disease in the United States Since 1880* (New York: Oxford University Press, 1987 [1985]).
12. Judith Walkowitz, *Prostitution in Victorian Society: Women, Class, and the State* (Cambridge: Cambridge University Press, 1980), p. 1.
13. Ruth Rosen, *The Lost Sisterhood: Prostitution in America, 1900–1918* (Baltimore: Johns Hopkins University Press, 1982) p. 10.
14. Marianna Valverde, *The Age of Light, Soap, and Water: Moral Reform in English Canada, 1885–1925* (Toronto: McClelland & Stewart, 1991), pp. 81–82. Also see John McLaren, "'White Slavers': The Reform of Canada's Prostitution Laws and Patterns of Enforcement, 1900–1920," *Criminal Justice History* 8 (1987): 127, p. 127; Judith Fingard, *The Dark Side of Life in Victorian Halifax* (Porter's Lake, N.S.: Potterfield's Press, 1989), p. 109. On the regulation of prostitution in Montreal, see Andrée Levesque, "Étiendre le Red Light: Les Réformateurs et la prostitution à Montréal entre 1865 et 1925," *Urban History Review/Revue d'histoire Urbaine*, vol. 17, no. 3 (February 1989).
15. Lynn Bowen, *Boss Whistle: The Coal Miners of Vancouver Island Remember* (Lantzville, B.C.: Oolichan Press, 1992), p. 218.
16. Fingard, *The Dark Side*, p. 109.

17. McLaren, "White Slavers," p. 33.
18. As quoted in McLaren, "White Slavers," p. 33.
19. Wendy Mitchinson, "'For God, Home and Native Land': A Study in Nineteenth-Century Feminism" in *A Not Unreasonable Claim: Women and Reform in Canada, 1880's–1920's*, ed. Linda Kealey (Toronto: Women's Educational Press, 1979), p. 163.
20. *KN*, 29 October 1898.
21. *KN*, 12 November 1898.
22. Ibid. The licensing fee ended up being substantially less: $1,000 per year for a saloon, $750 for a hotel.
23. *KN*, 12 April 1899.
24. *KN*, 6 May 1899.
25. Report of S.B. Steele, May 1899, NAC, RCMP Records, v. 1444, f. 181, p. 3; *KN*, 12 April 1899.
26. *KN*, 12 April, 1899.
27. Charges of corruption in and mismanagement of the Gold Commissioners Office, liquor permits, and general "administrative ineptitude" provided the Conservative Opposition in Ottawa with an opportunity to criticize the Laurier government. David Morrison, *The Politics of the Yukon Territory, 1898–1909* (Toronto: University of Toronto Press, 1968).
28. Ogilvie to Officer Commanding NWMP, 15 January 1900, YA, YTR, CLB v. 77, p. 738, cited in Guest, "A History," p. 220.
29. Heaman to Ogilvie, 27 June 1900, YA, YGR Series 1, v. 9, f. 1443.
30. Smart to Heaman, 3 July 1900, YA, YGR Series 1, v. 9, f. 1443.
31. Mitchinson, "For God, Home and Native Land," p. 158; McLaren, "White Slavers," p. 30.
32. Sifton to Ogilvie, 14 August 1900, YA, YGR Series 1, v. 9, f. 1443.
33. Ogilvie to William Muloch, 22 May 1900, YA, YGR Series 1, v. 9, f. 1443.
34. Ogilvie to Sifton, 12 September 1900, YA, YGR Series 1, v. 9, f. 1443.
35. Ibid.
36. Smart to Ogilvie, 22 November 1900, YA, YGR Series 1, v. 9, f. 1443.
37. Ogilvie to F.C. Wade, n.d., YA, YTR, CLB, v. 77, p. 738, cited in Guest, "A History," p. 229.
38. Guest, "A History," p.230.
39. As cited in D. Morrison, *The Politics of the Yukon Territory*, p. 37.
40. Some of the complaints were that Sifton had insisted on the appointment of J.D. McGregor to act as the issuer of liquor licenses. Council had refused, however, since Superintendent Steele stated that McGregor (the former Inspector of Mines) had been tried for horse stealing. Subsequently, Sifton had arranged to send Steele to the Boer War to get rid of him. Further, Ogilvie stated that his

annual report had been returned to him with several changes, and he had been ordered to sign it. Finally, Ogilvie believed that the liquor permit system was controlled by Sifton for his own political profit. D. Morrison, *The Politics of the Yukon Territory*, p. 34.

41. Wood to Ogilvie, 5 November, 1900, NAC, RCMP Records, v. 3032, cited in Guest, "A History," p. 231.
42. *KN*, 25 November 1900.
43. *KN*, 17 August 1901.
44. Ibid. It was actually the NWMP who issued the order.

Chapter 6

1. *KN*, 30 September 1902. As Paul Craven asserts in his study of law and ideology in the Toronto Police Court (1850–1880), "no metaphor was used more persistently by the newspapers to describe the police court than that of the theatre." See Paul Craven, "Law and Ideology: The Toronto Police Court, 1850–1880," in *Forging a Consensus: Historical Essays on Toronto*, ed. D. Flaherty (Toronto: University of Toronto Press, 1984), p. 286.
2. *KN*, 6 December 1902.
3. *KN*, 21 October 1902.
4. *KN*, 21 October 1902.
5. YA, MSS 141, October 1902.
6. *KN*, 21 October 1902.
7. *KN*, 29 October 1902.
8. Jeffrey Adler, "Streetwalkers, Degraded Outcasts, and Good-For-Nothing Huzzies: Women and the Dangerous Class in Antebellum St. Louis," *Journal of Social History* 25 (Summer 1993): 738.
9. *KN*, 11 January 1902.
10. *KN*, 12 February 1902.
11. David Morrison, *The Politics of the Yukon Territory, 1898–1909* (Toronto: University of Toronto Press, 1968) p. 43.
12. Ibid, p. 44.
13. Ibid, p. 41.
14. Ibid, pp. 42, 44.
15. YA, GR Series 11, v. 1433, f. 6.
16. YA, GR Series 11, v. 1443, f. 6, 17 October 1902.
17. NAC, RG 18, v. 279, f. 633, 12 July 1904.
18. Ottawa to R.W. Scott, 9 September 1903, NAC, RG 18, v. 254, f. 246.
19. Ken S. Coates, *Best Left as Indians: Native-White Relations in the Yukon Territory, 1840–1973* (Montreal: McGill-Queen's University Press, 1991), p. 45.
20. As quoted in Coates, *Best Left as Indians*, p. 84.
21. J.R. Miller, *Skscrapers Hide the Heavens: A History of Indian-White*

Relations in Canada (Toronto: University of Toronto Press, 1991 [1989]), p. 191. The Indian Act of 1951 lifted the prohibition of Aboriginal consumption of alcohol. Miller, p. 221.

22. *KN*, 14 January 1902.
23. *KN*, 22 January 1902.
24. *KN*, 16 July 1898.
25. *New York Times*, 26 November 1898.
26. Coates, *Best Left as Indians*, p. 45. In her study of coal mines on Vancouver Island, Lynn Bowen documents the same occurence. Lynn Bowen, *Boss Whistle: The Coal Miners of Vancouver Island Remember* (Lantzville, B.C.: Oolichan Press, 1992), pp. 69–73. See also, Nancy Forestell, "'All That Glitters is not Gold': The Gendered Dimensions of Work, Family, and Community Life in the Northern Ontario Gold Mining Town of Timmins, 1909–1950," Ph. D dissertation, University of Toronto, 1993.
27. *Whitehorse Star*, 28 June 1902.
28. *Klondike Miner and Arctic Circle Herald*, Grand Forks, 30 November 1901, quoted in William Keith Hubbard, "The Klondike Gold Rush in Literature, 1896–1930," M.A. thesis, University of Western Ontario, 1969, p. 136.

Chapter 7

1. Ken S. Coates and William R. Morrison, *Land of the Midnight Sun: A History of the Yukon* (Edmonton: Hurtig Publishers, 1988) p. 147.
2. *KN*, 14 May 1903.
3. *San Francisco Examiner*, 6 October 1897, quoted in Hal Guest, "A History of Dawson City," Microfiche Report Series 181 (Ottawa: Parks Canada, 1985), p. 12.
4. Asst. Commissioner Wood to Commissioner, 22 April 1904, YA, YGR Series 1, v. 9, f. 1443.
5. James Pattullo to Arthur Wilson, 25 March 1907, YA, YGR Series 1, v. 9, f. 1443.
6. Wood to Acting Commissioner, 27 June 1908, YA, YGR Series 1, v. 9, f. 1443.
7. Wilson to Pattullo, 9 April 1907, YA, YGR Series 1, v. 9, f. 1443.
8. Ibid.
9. Proprietors to Minister of Justice, April 1907, YA, YGR Series 1, v. 9, f. 1443.
10. Pringle to Laurier, 31 July 1907, YA, GOV 1158 79/129.
11. Ibid.
12. Guest, "A History," pp. 240–42.
13. David Morrison, *The Politics of the Yukon Territory, 1898–1909* (Toronto: University of Toronto Press, 1968), p. 83.

14. Guest, "A History," p. 242.
15. D. Morrison, *The Politics of the Yukon Territory*, p. 86.
16. *Canadian Annual Review* (1908), quoted in D. Morrison, *The Politics of the Yukon Territory*, p. 87.
17. Guest, "A History," p. 241.
18. D. Morrison, *The Politics of the Yukon Territory*, p. 86.
19. Ibid.
20. Ibid.
21. Guest, "A History," p. 242.
22. Proprietors to Minister of Justice, April 1907, YA, YGR Series 1, v. 9, f. 1443.
23. Wood to Commissioner, 7 December 1907, YA, YGR Series 1, v. 9, f. 1443.
24. Frank Oliver to Commissioner Henderson, 6 December 1907, YA, YGR Series 1, v. 9, f. 1443.

Conclusion

1. Dinsdale was referring to historians Arthur Lower (who had actually resigned in 1961) and Donald Creighton. House of Commons *Debates*, 22 March 1962, p. 2061.
2. Ibid.
3. *Yukon News*, 25 September 1997.

Selected Bibliography

Abbreviations Used

KN *Klondike Nugget*
NAC National Archives of Canada
YTA Yukon Territorial Archives

Newspapers

Dawson Daily News. Selected articles, 1998–1908.
Klondike Nugget. Selected articles, 1898–1908.
Whitehorse Star. Selected articles, 1898–1908.

National Archives

Canada, House of Commons *Debates*, 1962.
Canada, *1901 Manuscript Census*
Canada, Royal Canadian Mounted Police Records, RG 18

Yukon Archives

(YGR) Yukon Government Record, Group 1, Series 1, Volume 9, File
    1443
(GOV) Government Document, 1431
(GR) Government Record, Series 11
(GOV) Government, 1158

Secondary Sources

Adler, Jeffrey. "Streetwalkers, Degraded Outcasts, and Good-For-Nothing Huzzies: Women and the Dangerous Class in Antebellum St. Louis." *Journal of Social History*, vol. 25 (Summer 1993).

Anderson, Benedict. *Imagined Communities: Reflections on the Origin and Spread of Nationalism*. London, 1991.

Berton, Pierre. *The Klondike Fever: The Life and Death of the Last Great Gold Rush*. New York: Carroll and Graf Publishers, 1958.

Bommes, Michael, and Patrick Wright. "'Charms of Residence': The Public and the Past." In *Making Histories: Studies in History-Writing and Politics*, ed. Richard Johnson et al. London, 1992.

Bowen, Lynn. *Boss Whistle: The Coal Miners of Vancouver Island Remember*. Lantzville, B.C.: Oolichan Press, 1992.

Brandt, Allan. *No Magic Bullet: A Social History of Venereal Disease in the United States Since 1880*. New York: Oxford University Press, 1987 [1985].

Butler, Anne M. *Daughters of Joy, Sisters of Mercy: Prostitutes in the American West, 1865-1890*. Chicago: University of Illinois Press, 1985.

Coates, Ken S., *Best Left as Indians: Native-White Relations in the Yukon Territory, 1840-1973*. Montreal: McGill-Queen's University Press, 1991.

Coates, Ken S. and William R. Morrison. *Land of the Midnight Sun: A History of the Yukon*. Edmonton: Hurtig Publishers, 1988.

Corrigan, Philip, and Derek Sayer. *The Great Arch: English State Formation as Cultural Revolution*. Oxford: 1985.

Craven Paul, "Law and Ideology: The Toronto Police Court, 1850-1880." In *Forging a Consensus: Historical Essays on Toronto*, ed. D. Flaherty. Toronto: University of Toronto Press, 1984.

Davis, Mary Lee. *Sourdough Gold: The Log of a Yukon Adventure*. Boston, 1933.

de la Cour, Lykke, Cecilia Morgan and Mariana Valverde. "Gender Regulation and State Formation." In *Colonial Leviathan: State Formation in Mid-Nineteenth Century Canada*. eds. Alan Greer and Ian Radforth. Toronto: University of Toronto Press, 1992.

D'Emilio, John, and Estelle Freedman. *Intimate Matters: A History of Sexuality in America*. New York: Harper and Row, 1988.

Dubinsky, Karen. *Improper Advances: Rape and Heterosexual Conflict in Ontario, 1880-1929*. Chicago: University of Chicago Press, 1993.

——. "'The Pleasure is Exquisite but Violent': The Imaginary Geography of Niagara Falls in the Nineteenth Century." *Journal of Canadian Studies*, vol. 29, no. 2 (Summer 1994).

——, and Franca Iacovetta. "Murder, Womanly Virtue, and Motherhood: The Case of Angelina Napolitano, 1911-1922." *Canadian Historical Review*, vol. 72, 1991.

Fetherling, Douglas. *The Gold Crusades: A Social History of Gold Rushes, 1849-1929*. Toronto: Macmillan, 1988.

Fingard, Judith. *The Dark Side of Life in Victorian Halifax*. Porter's Lake, N.S.: Pottersfield Press, 1989.

Fisher, Robin. *Duff Pattullo of British Columbia*. Toronto: University of Toronto Press, 1991.

Forestell, Nancy. "'All That Glitters is Not Gold': The Gendered Dimensions of Work, Family, and Community Life in the Northern Ontario Gold Mining Town of Timmins, 1909-1950." Ph.D. dissertation: University of Toronto, 1993.

Gates, Michael. *Gold at Fortymile Creek: Early Days in the Yukon*. Vancouver: University of British Columbia Press, 1994.

Gilfoyle, Timothy. *City of Eros: New York City, Prostitution and the Commercialization of Sex, 1790-1920*. New York and London: W.W. Norton and Company, 1992.

Goldman, Marion S. *Gold Diggers and Silver Miners: Prostitution and Social Life on the Comstock Lode*. Ann Arbor: University of Michigan Press, 1981.

Gordon, Linda, and Joan Scott. "Debates." *Signs*, 15, no. 4 (Summer 1990): 848-60.

Gray, James H. *Red Lights on the Prairies.* Toronto: Macmillan of Canada, 1971.

Guest, Hal. "Dawson City, San Francisco of the North or Boomtown in a Bog: A Literature Review." Manuscript Report Series 241. Ottawa: Parks Canada, 1978.

——."A History of Dawson City." Microfiche Report Series 181. Ottawa: Parks Canada, 1985.

Hall, D.J. *Clifford Sifton: The Young Napoleon, 1861-1900.* Vancouver: University of British Columbia Press, 1981.

Hamilton, Roberta. "Feminist Theories." *left history*, vol. 1, no. 1 (Spring 1993).

Hubbard, William Keith. "The Klondike Gold Rush in Literature, 1896-1930." M.A. thesis: University of Western Ontario, 1969.

Johnston, Susan. "Twice Slain: Female Sex Trade Workers and Suicide in British Columbia, 1870-1920." Paper presented to the annual conference of the Canadian Historical Association, Calgary, June 1994.

Kealey, Linda, ed. *A Not Unreasonable Claim: Women and Reform in Canada, 1880's-1920's.* Toronto: Women's Educational Press, 1979.

Kelcey, Barbara. "Lost in the Rush: The Forgotten Women of the Klondike Gold Rush." M.A. thesis. University of Victoria, 1987.

Kinsman, Gary. *The Regulation of Desire: Sexuality in Canada.* Montreal: Black Rose Books, 1987.

Levesque, Andrée. "Étiendre le Red Light: Les Réformateurs et la prostitution à Montréal entre 1865 et 1925." *Urban History Review*, vol. 17, no. 3 (February 1989).

Mangan, J.A., and James Walvin, eds. *Manliness and Morality: Middle-Class Masculinity in Britain and America, 1800-1940.* Manchester: Manchester University Press, 1987.

Mayer, Melanie. *Klondike Women: True Tales of the 1897-1898 Gold Rush*. Swallow Press/Ohio University Press, 1989.

Maynard, Steven. "Rough Work and Rugged Men: The Social Construction of Masculinity in Working-Class History." *Labour/ Le Travail*, vol. 23 (1989).

McClellan, Catherine. *Part of the Land, Part of the Water: A History of the Yukon Indians*. Vancouver: Douglas & McIntyre, 1987.

McHugh, Paul. *Prostitution and Victorian Social Reform*. London: Croom Helm, 1980.

McKay, Ian. "Among the Fisherfolk: J.F.B. Livesay and the Invention of Peggy's Cove." *Journal of Canadian Studies*, vol. 23 (Spring/ Summer 1988).

McLaren, John. "Chasing the Social Evil: Moral Fervour and the Evolution of Canada's Prostitution Laws, 1867-1917." *Canadian Journal of Law and Society*, vol. 1 (1986).

———. "'White Slavers': The Reform of Canada's Prostitution Laws and Patterns of Enforcement, 1900-1920." *Criminal Justice History* 8 (1987): 125-65.

Mitchinson, Wendy. "'For God, Home and Native Land': A Study in Nineteenth-Century Feminism." In *A Not Unreasonable Claim: Women and Reform in Canada, 1880's-1920's*, ed. Linda Kealey (Toronto: Women's Educational Press, 1979.

Morrison, David. *The Politics of the Yukon Territory, 1898-1909*. Toronto: University of Toronto Press, 1968.

Morrison, William. *Showing the Flag: The Mounted Police and Canadian Sovereignty in the North, 1894-1925*. Vancouver: University of British Columbia Press, 1985.

———. "Policing the Boomtown: The Mounted Police as a Social Force in the Klondike." *Northern Review* (Winter 1990).

Murphy, Mary. "The Private Lives of Public Women: Prostitution in Butte, Montana, 1878-1917." In *The Women's West*, ed. Susan Armitage and Elizabeth Jameson. Norman: University of Oklahoma Press, 1987.

Neufeld, David, and Frank Norris. *Chilkoot Trail: Heritage Route to the Klondike*. Whitehorse: Lost Moose Publishers, 1997.

Parr, Joy. *The Gender of Breadwinners*. Toronto: University of Toronto Press, 1990.

Peiss, Kathy. *Cheap Amusements: Working Women and Leisure in Turn-of-the-Century New York*. Philadelphia: Temple University Press, 1986.

———, and Christina Simmons with Robert Padug. *Passion and Power: Sexuality in History*. Philadelphia: Temple University Press, 1989.

Petrak, Paula. *No Step Backwards: Women and Family on the Rocky Mountain Mining Frontier, Helena, Montana, 1865-1900*. Helena: Montana Historical Society Press, 1987.

Roper, Michael, and John Tosh. *Manful Assertions: Masculinity in Britain Since 1800*. London: Routledge, 1991.

Rosen, Ruth. *The Lost Sisterhood: Prostitution in America, 1900-1918*. Baltimore: Johns Hopkins University Press, 1982.

Rotenberg, Lori. "The Wayward Worker: Toronto's Prostitute at the Turn of the Century." In *Women at Work in Ontario, 1850-1936*, ed. Janice Acton, Penny Goldsmith, and Bonnie Shepard. Toronto: Women's Educational Press, 1974.

Scott, Joan. "Gender: A Useful Category of Historical Analysis." In *Gender and the Politics of History*. New York, 1988.

Shields, Rob. *Places on the Margin: Alternative Geographies of Modernity*. London: Routledge, 1991.

Stansell, Christine. *City of Women: Sex and Class in New York, 1789-1860*. Urbana and Chicago: University of Illinois Press, 1987.

Stone, Thomas. "Urbanism, Law, and Public Order: A View from the Klondike." In *For Purposes of Dominion: Essays in Honour of Morris Zaslow*, ed. Ken Coates and William Morrison. North York, O.N.: Captus Press, 1989.

Strange, Carolyn. "The Perils and Pleasures of the City: Single, Wage-Earning Women in Toronto, 1880-1930." Ph.D dissertation: Rutgers, 1991.

Stuart, Richard. "Recycling Used Boom Towns: Dawson and Tourism." *Northern Review*, vol. 6 (Winter 1990).

Taylor, C.J. *Negotiating the Past: The Making of Canada's National Historic Parks and Sites.* Montreal: McGill-Queen's University Press, 1990.

Urry, John. *The Tourist Gaze: Leisure and Travel in Contemporary Societies.* Lincoln: University of Nebraska Press, 1985.

Valverde, Mariana. *The Age of Light, Soap, and Water: Moral Reform in English Canada, 1885-1925.* Toronto: McClelland & Stewart, 1991.

Valverde, Mariana, and Lorna Weir. "The Struggles of the Immoral: Preliminary Remarks on Moral Regulation." *Resources for Feminist Research*, vol. 17 (September 1988).

Van Kirk, Sylvia. "A Vital Presence: Women in the Cariboo Gold Rush, 1862-1875." In *B.C. Reconsidered: Essays on Women*, ed. Veronica Strong-Boag and Gillian Creese. Vancouver: Press Gang Publishers, 1992.

Walkowitz, Judith. *Prostitution and Victorian Society: Women, Class, and the State.* New York: Cambridge University Press, 1980.

Appendix

Select Criminal Convictions, Yukon Territory, 1900–1903
1901 Census of Canada

	1900		1901		1902		1903	
	M	F	M	F	M	F	M	F
Vagrancy	9		25	1	54	5	31	
Drunkenness	34		355	15	731	26	328	9
Indecent Exposure				2		5		
Insulting, Obscene and Profane Language				2		13	2	
Keeping, Frequenting Bawdy Houses and Inmates Thereof			2	43	18	85	3	30
Loose, Idle, Disorderly	14		4		38		12	2
Total Convictions (all criminal offenses)	1862	1	1174	85	1868	146	834	88

(Statistics not available prior to 1900)

Index

Bay Ryley is a writer and editor from Toronto. Her four summers spent in Whitehorse, Yukon captured her interest in the infamous can-can girl and prompted this book. Ryley is currently studying law at Dalhousie University.